Aurea Vidyā Collection

—————— 6 ——————

*For a complete list of Titles see page 145

Orphism and the Initiatory Tradition

This book was originally published in Italian as,
Raphael, *Orfismo e Tradizione Iniziatica*. Associazione Ecoculturale
Parmenides (formerly Edizioni Āśram Vidyā). Rome

First published in English in 2003
by Aurea Vidyā
39 West 88th Street, New York, N.Y. 10024, U.S.A.
www.vidya-ashramvidyaorder.org

ISBN 978-1-931406-05-5

Library of Congress Control Number: 2003101018

On the cover: Orphic Gold Tablet, V - IV Century B.C., found in
Hipponion (Vibo Valentia), Italy.
Museo Archeologico di Vibo Valentia, Italy.
(English translation on page 135)

Raphael

(Āśram Vidyā Order)

Orphism
and the
Initiatory Tradition

Aurea Vidyā

If the hammer of the sensorial demon has shut your eyelids and closed your ears, come! I shall give you the light to see the symbols of Beauty and the hearing to capture the magical sound of the Spirit.

Raphael

CONTENTS

Dionysus! This name has been on the lips of thousands of people in different places since time out of mind; and if it continues to be written, this means that He is still present.

Herodotus traces his origin to Egypt, others to Thrace, Lydia, or Phrygia; yet others to Crete, where tablets dating to the fifteenth century before Christ have been found bearing the names of Dionysus and 'The Lady of the Labyrinth', meaning Ariadne.

Homer, too, refers to Dionysus, even before most of the Greeks acknowledged him as the Saviour. It should be accepted that behind specific names there lies a universal Principle; in fact, all Traditions - East and West, North and South - speak of divine figures which, in short, equate to each other, as do what we usually call 'myths'.

Demeter, for example, is the equivalent of Isis; and Dionysus, of Osiris. Thus the Egyptian Isis and Osiris comprise a 'myth' which is the same as that of the Greek Demeter and Dionysus.

The Babylonian religion and the Assyrian religion use different names which are equivalent to Demeter and Dionysus; they also have the same 'myth' concerning the death and re-birth of their god.

So there are 'myths' and names which do not belong to any specific people or individual, simply because, as

we have said above, they represent universal Principles or
Ideas (in the Platonic sense).

Historians and ethnologists strive to discover whether a
specific 'myth' or divinity is related to a specific people,
just as many historians of philosophy are at pains to show,
for example, that the philosophy of Pythagoras, Parmenides,
Plato, Plotinus, and others is a purely personal one that
has not been adopted from other thinkers but developed
by the mind/intuition of the 'originator'. In the view of all
these historians, to think of Dionysus, Isis, the *Mahādevī* of
India, or even Pythagoras, Plato, and so on, in terms which
are quite impersonal or beyond nationality, is to devalue
the actual intuition of those people or those founders of
'myths'. Different orthodox historians seek to *individualise*
knowledge by erecting an altar to the individual creator
of 'systems', be they religious, philosophical, or scientific.

But if one is able to get close to what these minds
have said, and transcend individualistic and frequently
parochial attitudes, one can acknowledge, without fear of
going astray, that the essence, the theme, and the noumenon
are identical in all traditional philosophies, religions, and
systems of knowledge. Every being, then, according to its
level of consciousness and intuitive/contemplative awakening, re-clothes this essence with richness and beauty of
form, but most of all with the power of its own irradiation.

For example, the Philosophy of Plato, notwithstanding
its enthusiastic champions and its bitter critics, will always
remain a milestone and a foundation of philosophical science and spiritual mysticism.

If all the different 'myths' and all the essences of the
various philosophies have profound analogies and even
identity, it means that Truth is one and single and that
this Truth is of an order that is not individual but supra-
individual and supra-sensible and therefore traditional.

This is the very meaning of traditional Truth, Teaching, Doctrine, and so on. Tradition is not based on individual opinion but on noetic intellection. For if Truth were purely individual, it would not be universal Truth, valid for all, for every individual would represent a self-contained truth, and it would be absurd to claim that one individual could comprehend another individual/truth whose nature could not possibly coincide with the nature of the former individual/ truth. This would give rise to the well-known expressions 'Tower of Babel' and 'confusion of tongues'. If we are able to understand each other and entertain ideas which are related, analogous, and even identical, it means that within us there is something which links us, unifies us, and joins us to a *single* common denominator. According to the divine Plato and Parmenides himself - to cite only two great Philosophers - the world of sensible individu- alities represents nothing more than a world of *opinion*, not a world of *knowledge* or science. And if opinion is subjective, individual, and sense-based, then knowledge/sci- ence must belong to another dimension, another existential sphere which can be accessed. And if knowledge belongs to the supra-sensible realm, then it is not the prerogative of the individual as such, or of a people or of a histori- cal period; it is therefore traditional. And again, if 'myth' is nothing other than knowledge expressed in a particular symbolic form, because it is acknowledged that supreme Truth cannot be conceptualised or demonstrated empiri- cally, then 'myth' has a value that is universal and not individual and particular.

'Myth is a fragmented image of the truth, just as the rainbow is the reflection of the light of the sun, whose rays are refracted in the cloud. But one can gather and re-assemble the pieces of this broken mirror so as to reconstitute it.'[1]

'Aristotle himself acknowledges the philosophical function of myth in the initial pages of his *Metaphysics* (A2, 982b 18), his actual words being, "Even he who loves myth is in some way a philosopher".'[2]

And Severino writes, 'Myth is not intended to be something devised by the imagination, but the revelation of the essential and comprehensive meaning of the world. Even in the Greek language the oldest meaning of the word *mýthos* is 'word', 'saying', 'statement'. Sometimes *mýthos* means even 'the thing itself', 'reality'. Only in a derivative way, and much later in the Greek language, does *mýthos* come to suggest 'legend', 'fable', 'tale', and 'myth'.'[3]

And what can those people mean who have written or said things which the average mortal cannot even imagine? For those few who transcend reductive individualism, such people – Philosophers, Mystics, Religious people, and so on – are the *mediators* between the intelligible and the sensible. They are ready or able, through their high level of consciousness, to reveal, within time and space, aspects of noetic Truth, to rectify[4] the possible decline of this Truth, and to stimulate and exalt, not individuality, but the slumbering consciousness of humanity itself. For these few, they – more than mere individualities who create 'original' religious or philosophical systems – are

---

[1] Plutarch, *How to Study Poetry*, X.

[2] G. Reale, *Storia della filosofia antica*, Vol. V. Vita e Pensiero. Milan.

[3] E. Severino, *La filosofia antica*. Rizzoli. Milan.

[4] Rectify: to put or set right, to remedy, (Alchemy) to purify or refine. Oxford English Dictionary. See the Chapter 'Rectifying the common fires (*nigredo*) and Fixing the philosophical Mercury' in *The Threefold Pathway of Fire* by Raphael. Aurea Vidyā, New York.

the *bridges* by which those who are qualified can regain the return pathway to their Homeland. For these few, an Orpheus, a Pythagoras, a Parmenides, a Plato, a Plotinus, and so on, are not a Locke, a Hume, a Fichte, and so on, however great a stimulus these latter might be to the mind and conceptualisation.

To say that the Philosophy of Pythagoras, Parmenides, Plato, and so on, belongs to the *Philosophia perennis* because it is not, in fact, individual and limited by time is not to detract from their personality. Far from it, for this is to acknowledge them as 'mediators', 'divine transmitters', or *avatāras*, as they would be called in the East.

If one could comprehend the Philosophy of Plato in its essence and realise it in practice, one would undoubtedly reach the point of transfiguring one's own being.[1]

Plato's Philosophy is Metaphysics based on a supraontological Principle, a theology, an ontology, a *mysticism*, and an ethic which is both individual and social: all of which take practical form in an authentic teaching which is initiatory in the widest sense of the word.

And Orpheus? What can we say of this great Sage, Magus, Theologian, Innovator, Rectifier; this *ṛṣi*, to use the word from *Vedānta*? As the following pages will seek to show, Orpheus is another mediator/bridge, a great *avatāra*, who rectified the cult of Dionysus which had deteriorated and had become superstition; revealed Truth of an intelligible and Apollonian order; devised a science of Rite and Number by means of music; instituted the Mysteries, both the Lesser and the Greater; left behind him, under the aegis of Apollo [ά-πόλλων = not many], an impression, a vibration, an influence of such magnitude that they can

---

[1] On this aspect, see *Initiation into the Philosophy of Plato* by Raphael. Aurea Vidyā, New York.

still be felt today. Furthermore, he exerted a considerable
influence on the minds of the philosophers of ancient
Greece and therefore on all subsequent philosophers.

What can we say of Orpheus? Little or much: it depends on the perspective we wish to adopt. But it would
be better not to speak of *vibrating consciousnesses* such
as his, and instead try to grasp, through noetic intuition
or pure *contemplation*, their 'state' of consciousness and
to be able, by raising oneself through the various levels of
contemplation, to reach the point of being 'face to face'
with It, the Good, indivisible unity.

The Mysteries instituted by the divine Orpheus represent various *states of being*, and the neophyte, rather than
proceeding in a discursive manner to prove empirically
what cannot be proved, is required to adopt the right
psychological attitude and level of consciousness for being
able to enter the 'tabernacle' of the Mystery and merge
and be established there.

There are some things which, not being mere phenomena to observe and catalogue, are not subject to scientific or
conceptual empirical proof, but can be *consciously* realised.

> 'Unlike other types of knowledge, this type cannot in
> fact be communicated at all by words, but after *long
> familiarity* centred on the subject, and after *living*
> with it, *on the instant* - like a spark flying from a
> palpitating flame - it rises in the soul and nourishes
> itself by itself.'[1]

In the few pages that follow, an attempt will be made
to show, directly or indirectly, how 'certain things' are
supra-historical, how they belong to a single Source; how
one can be 'reconciled' with oneself and others through

---

[1] Plato, *Seventh Letter*, 341 c-d. (Italics are ours).

turning to this single *Source*; how some 'myths' concerning people and events are not dead but merely sleeping; and how it would take almost nothing to bring them back into the light of the sun if only one had the inspiration which comes from this *Source*.

It is undoubtedly the case that people who draw inspiration from this single *Source* can recognise each other at the level of the sensible world on account of factors which make them obvious. Here are just a few of these factors:

1. First and foremost is the factor of *living, embodying*, and *vibrating* the single *Source*. It is important to distinguish the skilful 'speakers' from the humble, vibrating consciousnesses, and this involves *comprehending*, taking into oneself, integrating, all possible points of view.

2. Having that composure, reserve, and humility (in its true meaning) which are the characteristics of one who possesses certain qualities.

3. Avoiding controversies, judgements, and sophistry, even when the 'spiritual multitude' put forward *opinions* (all the others pose no problem, since they are far removed from certain perspectives). This factor is the result of transcending the empirical or relational mind.

4. Having that *level of Dignity*[1] which indicates transcendence of one's own subconsciousness and the collective subconsciousness, as well as the mastery of the energies/qualities of substance or χώρα, to use Plato's word.

---

[1] Cf. 'Sulphurous Dignity' in the Chapter 'Fire of Life', *The Threefold Pathway of Fire* by Raphael, op. cit.

5. Revealing these Truths which pertain to specific realms of Being. This is very important, for the words that are *written* or *spoken* and the life that is *lived* provide an understanding of whether the Inspired Person comes from the single Source or from heterogeneous and even individualised sources, even if these express contents of value. From what is written and spoken, and from the way one lives, it is possible to understand whether qualities/faculties of individuality – however elevated – are being expressed or whether it is the *Source* itself which lives and manifests itself in the Philosopher.

Most people, including those who are considered to be *great*, even by advanced minds, express only individualised faculties/qualities that have been well practised. Nor is it the quantity of words or writings which denotes a connection to the single *Source*.

One who draws inspiration from the single *Source* has a mark which is unmistakeable and indescribable, but which will not easily escape the notice of anyone who experiences the joyful Secret of his own heart. These Inspired People have different levels of maturity, and each one *consciously* develops his own function in the large context, both subtle and coarse/physical, of the universal network.

The various significant passages which have been quoted from outstanding writers in connection with Orpheus and Orphism are ones with which the Author of this book is in complete harmony.

Aurea Vidyā

INTRODUCTION

The Author of this book acknowledges that he has merely touched the surface of the issue of the Sacred Mysteries and the events that have characterised the life of Orpheus. On the other hand, it is not his task to expatiate on a problem that would not provide any advantage but would simply serve to satisfy empirical intellective curiosity.

The Author has never written or spoken for the many, but for those few who, once the fire has been kindled within them, know how to feed it until it becomes a huge flame of *love for Knowledge/Realisation*.

The present era in the history of humanity is characterised by an intense numbness of consciousnesses and a strong focus of attention upon the sphere of the *physical* and *sensible*: these absorb all the energies.

Even those 'many' who are interested in matters of spirituality, religion, or initiation tend to put the main emphasis on the contingent and particular aspect, even if they express themselves in terms of transcending the empirical or simply of realisative metaphysics.

Some, and they are by no means few, are then troubled by psychological problems, environmental maladjustment, and various frustrations, as a result of which they have recourse to *yoga* or Western esoteric literature simply as a means of relief or therapy.

Yet others – and we shall go no further – follow teachings which can help to release latent feelings of passive
devotionalism, sexual energy or psychic power (*siddhi*);
indeed, they even attempt to make these factors more
powerful to gratify their own mundane needs.

The original teachings of the *ṛṣis,* of Śaṅkara, Orpheus,
Hermes, Plato, Plotinus, Buddha, and of Jesus Himself,
have, in the eyes of the 'profane[1] spiritualist', lost their
Dignity, Authority, Austerity: their true and authentic
essence. Their teachings are commercialised, degraded,
twisted, and interpreted in such a way as to enable the
'empirical ego' to find its own space and its own survival.

'To polish one's own rough stone' is hard work, especially nowadays, because, after all, it turns out to be easier
to delegate the task to others. The state of humanity in the
current 'iron age' is such that it seems difficult to effect
even a simple *rectification.* However, there is no cause for
despair, because dejection and despair are part of *avidyā*
(metaphysical ignorance) or emotional fog. In the world of
becoming, everything is cyclical: birth, growth, decay, and
then one starts again. This cyclical process has endured
since the beginning of time, and so there is nothing to
wonder at: everything is in its rightful place.

Those who feel a sense of responsibility, who hear the
call of the Soul to a life of transfiguration, who are deaf to
the allurements of worldly power, erudite opinion, criticism
for exalting or demolishing others, who truly wish to strip
themselves of their egoic trappings, are undoubtedly able, if
they also feel humble and trusting, to *prepare themselves*

---

[1] See, *The Philosophy of Being* by Raphael, Aurea Vidyā, New York,
page 28:

'...Following these introductory remarks, we may say that science is
profane; that is, it sees things from a point of view which is general and
phenomenal but not absolute.'

for the time when traditional *Truth* will arise, that *Truth* which by its own nature, can never be defeated by the *opinion* of the many, even were the majority of mankind to perish in some colossal cataclysm.

On the other hand, *one who knows* cannot be disturbed by possible catastrophes, because he comprehends what they might symbolise in the great game of cosmic becoming.

The human being, as such, must acknowledge that he is composed of two elements: the titanic (to use an Orphic word) and the divine. It is for each consciousness to establish whether to unite with the divine or with the titanic. The individual is an element of transition, by means of which he is everything and nothing. His struggle, his toil, his very impotence come from not knowing how to *define* himself and consequently from not knowing how to unify and integrate himself. But fortunately this ambiguity is not absolute, because the titanic element is only a 'superimposition' on pure Reality, although this superimposition can assume such a thickness and consistency that it is taken to be real. No one will ever be able to destroy the Divinity which is within the human being, for it is an intrinsic part of his nature. The titanic factor is a second false nature which, as was noted earlier, can be made apparently stable by the creative force of the mind. At the present time humanity lives so completely under the stamp of this false nature as to be its defenceless prisoner. Truth has been turned on its head: what *appears* is real, and what really is is false.

If these 'few' *definitely* know how to detach themselves from this hypnotic covering, and also from the opium of alibis, and if they dare oppose the oppressive ghost of the 'golden calf', which the titanic element knows how to present with masterly skill, and if they can set aside their individual interests and profane ideologies, then they will be able to *prepare themselves* for future events. The single *Source* knows how to wait, for it is outside time and space.

The disciple of today, be he in the metaphysical realm or a *kṣatriya*, must be a warrior; and if lacks determination, daring, unshakeable decision, and single-minded direction, no matter how much interest he has in initiatory matters, no matter how well he performs his morning meditation, no matter how ably he writes some essay for the edification of others, or attends literary, philosophical, or religious groups, the fact remains that he differs not a jot from the masses who experience the narcotic effects of illusion and nihilism.

It is good to recall that what has died with regard to Hermes, Orpheus, Gautama, Śaṅkara, Pythagoras, Plato, and others, is only the physical instrument, their shadow, their 'prison', and not what they have expressed and bequeathed to mankind. And this is what matters. That one day one or other of them may appear again, with a different name and a different mental and physical make-up, is of little importance. Name and form do not count (however much some aspirants defend only the name and form of their Masters); what counts is the spirit of Truth and the propulsive, irradiating force which such beings can vibrate and transmit.

To those 'few' who can summon up the strength to face the ghost of illusion and mistiness, a word of encouragement: one who is on the way (ὁδός is the word used by Parmenides)[1] will never be alone.

R.

---

[1] For ὁδός, see Parmenides, *On the Order of Nature*, edited by Raphael. Aurea Vidyā, New York.

HOMER, HESIOD, ORPHEUS

Greek society of the 9th and 8th centuries B.C. is characterised by the expression of an anthropomorphic polytheism such as we find particularly in the Homeric epics.

The gods and goddesses are mere idealisations conceived in the image of man. They are individuals who, in an expanded form, possess qualities and pursue activities which pertain expressly to man. Each of these individuals has his or her precise existential status and personal connotations, as well as specific formal appearance. Each divinity presides over natural phenomena and meddles with them according to its own emotional disposition, although there are limits, for it is subject to an overriding power known as Fate or Moira.

In the Homeric poems, however, one can already trace the outlines of a hierarchy of gods, with Zeus standing at their head. This need for a divine hierarchy gradually becomes ever more evident until the stage is reached where a Theogony and a cosmology are created.

The Theogony of Hesiod, of whom we shall speak more in due course, represents the paradigm[1] of this tendency.

The highest qualities manifested by the *heroes* – courage, physical vigour, astuteness, daring, and so on – are attributed, in the Homeric poems, to the gods, but, as we have noted before, in a rather exaggerated way. Thus

---

[1] *Paradigm* (παράδειγμα): in Platonic metaphysical terminology this word means the 'model' on which sensible things are structured.

the hierarchy of the gods, with Zeus at the head, and their inter-relationships are nothing but a reproduction of the organisation found in human society. What counts in the 'Homeric religion' is heroism, struggle, and a hero's death on earth.

'In Homer,' writes V. Cilento - 'the after-life is not the immortality of the *Phaedo*, but is found within the world itself as fame and glory, the songs of the bards and one's name on the lips of men and women. Heroism and immortality complete the feeling of tragedy, and a great Mediterranean light encompasses Homer's Divinities, powerful statues in which the religion of Achilles is mirrored. It is not a religion for the humble ... In the *Iliad* scorn is heaped upon the few of humble birth, such as Thersites and Dolo. This is because, for the Achaean warriors, they are less than men. The others – the heroes – are demi-gods, because, in the words of Pindar (*Nemean* VI. 1) "men and gods come from the same stock.""[1]

This conception of life is not expressed as an educational and ethical standard for the people. The heroes are the few, so that, as Lamanna observes, 'Awareness of the dependence of human life on the will and power of the gods is not translated – in the spirit of the Homeric Man – into an ethical vision of life or a conception of a moral code for human activity. The will of the gods is capricious and readily subject to provocation: and through Destiny, that force by which it is limited, it unfolds for men an action which is blind and makes no distinction between good and bad in assigning each one his lot. There is no idea of justice in the next world: the punishments meted out by the gods are merely their revenge upon those men

---

[1] V. Cilento, "La mistica ellenica", in *La mistica non cristiana*. Morcelliana, Brescia.

who have dared to oppose their capricious and biased will. What man asks from the gods is purely the attainment of his egoistic ends, and even prayer and sacrifice have the egoistic character of a real contract."[1]

A similar view of life could justifiably be held of an order that is naturalistic, immanentist, and very close to what might be defined as a materialistic view of existence.

Reale writes: 'But when Pythagoras speaks of "transmigration of souls", and Heraclitus speaks of "a destiny beyond this earth for the soul", and Empedocles explains the life of "purification", naturalism is seriously undermined, *and this undermining cannot be comprehended without having recourse to the religion of the Mysteries and in particular to Orphism.*'[2]

A separate discussion could be given with regard to the Theogony of Hesiod (8th century B.C.), because it, too, contains something traditional.

The moral law which Hesiod expounds, for example, in *Works and Days* is in stark contrast to that of Homer. In the Homeric vision, as we have already seen, the only qualities that are exalted are the strength, power, and heroism which are outside all moral law, for even the gods are passionate, easily provoked, revengeful, and thus incapable of holding an impartial and constant attitude. In Hesiod's vision, on the other hand, there flourishes a moral law which is the same for all and which is the direct expression of Zeus, who transcends all human passion and standard of conduct.

[1] E. P. Lamanna, *Storia della filosofia antica*, vol. I, "Il pensiero antico". Le Monnier, Florence.

[2] E. P. Lamanna, *Storia della filosofia antica*, vol. I, op. cit.

In contrast to the irresponsible justice of the kings who 'devour gifts', Hesiod puts forward the 'right judgements and impartial verdict' of Zeus:

> 'One who harms others effects his own harm ... .
> When the eye of Zeus, who sees everything, chooses,
> it rests on such happenings and knows what is just
> within our city. If the unjust man receives rewards from
> justice, then it is absurd for a just person to pursue
> justice. I do not believe, however, that the wise Zeus
> can do things like this.'[1]

According to Hesiod, the punishment due to an unjust man – be he king or humble citizen – does not take long to fall.

Robin writes: 'In the Homeric poems, the power of Zeus was the instrument of a capricious will that was easily provoked, or of that Moira whose incomprehensible activity serves to oppose or deceive our wish to be just. In Hesiod, the power of Zeus is the decree of a consciousness which judges, rightly and impartially, in accordance with the regulation or measure which it has determined, and metes out a dreadful punishment, not only to anyone who has transgressed it but also to anyone who has stooped low enough to become an accomplice in the offence. It is this which brought about the downfall of the "silver age" and which will ruin the "iron age". Now the essential principle of all the offences which are committed against the supreme law is the absence of measure or the desire to put oneself above order or rule ... . Hesiod, on the other hand, fervently believes in the existence of a law for the weak; and the specific task of omnipotent Zeus is to restore rectitude and measure.'[2]

---

[1]   Hesiod, *Works and Days*, 265-273

[2]   E. P. Lamanna, *Storia della filosofia antica*, vol. I, op. cit.

As far as the Theogony is concerned, Hesiod also re-introduces into it the cosmogonical aspect.

Before all else, he seeks inspiration from the Muses, because they know the Truth, speak to intelligence, declare the laws governing all things, and reveal the principle of everything. The steps in this Theogony are shown in the following hierarchical sequence:

Chaos —> Erebus and Night —> Ether and Day —>
Earth —> Starry Heaven —> Mountain and Sea (Pontus) —>
Ocean —-> Chronos and Rhea —-> Zeus

Hesiod wishes to show here how a line of transmission runs through manifestation; how there is a subordinate hierarchical relationship; how each element constitutes an essential link in the great universal scheme; and how organisation is effected within a system of stable relationships.

With Hesiod, therefore, there is an effort to translate traditional thought into cognitive terms.

The Greeks of that time, however, did not yet have sacred Teachings, revealed books, or priestly castes to preserve and protect a Tradition. The Homeric poems and Hesiod's Theogony were the only sources of inspiration. They represented the dominant 'public religion'. But the fact that the *Establishment* of the Orphic Mysteries could be, could have happened, shows that the Homeric religion had lost its function, its bite; or rather, it needs to be acknowledged that the moment had come to transform a mere belief into a realisable initiatory vision.

The figure of Orpheus has its place in this context of transformation and renewal of men's consciousness.

In relation to Orphism, Reale writes: 'His message – re-considered in various ways – *constitutes the central reference point for much of Greek philosophical thought*

... Now, without Orphism we would not be able to ex-plain Pythagoras, Heraclitus, Empedocles, or, of course, Plato himself and all that comes from him ... . And it will be precisely the strong call of the Orphic Vision that will prompt Plato to undertake his "second voyage" ["τὸν δεύτεϱον πλοῦν", *Phaedo*, 99D], that is, to follow that way which will lead him to the discovery of the supra-sensible world."[1]

This is the same as saying that the creation of a metaphysical view of Being in Europe originates princi-pally in Orphism, with its exposition of real Being which *transcends nature.*

It is good to mention at this point that even Thales and the other philosophers who expounded *physis*[2] in the 6th and 5th centuries are indebted to Orphism, which had already made mention in its cosmogony of the four elements which form the basis of the manifest universe.

It will be remembered that Thales, like Democritus himself, has his philosophical and scientific outlook formed in the temples of Egypt and Chaldea.

Another line of thought may be mentioned, one that became intertwined with the Homeric line of thought and at the same time diverged from it: a line of thought char-acterised by initiation rites, worship, symbols, and popular festivals, with tendencies to sanctify particular acts and to raise the consciousness of the initiates.

This cult, which was practised at Eleusis, was in honour of Demeter, Goddess of 'Mother Earth', to whom a 'myth' was attributed: Persephone, Demeter's daughter,

---

[1]   E. P. Lamanna, *Storia della filosofia antica*, vol. I, op. cit. (Italics are Reale's, the editor. The square brackets are ours).

[2]   The philosophy of *physis* is a search to identify that thing out of which all else is derived and to which it will ultimately return (the source and origin of the world).

was seized and taken underground, where she was forced to spend the whole winter, but in spring she was allowed to be with her mother in Olympus.

Beneath this innocent mythical account, however, is concealed a precise initiatory symbolism.

Another cult, more solar but also esoteric, prevalent from the 8th century B.C., was in honour of Apollo in the sanctuary of Delphi. These two sanctuaries, like the ones at Olympia, Thebes, and elsewhere, were to become famous by emitting a specific spiritual influence, especially through Orphism.

Some sources state that Musaeus (Μουσαῖος), prophet, priest, and direct follower of Orpheus (followed by Musaeus' son, Eumolpus, who would continue his father's work) anchored the Mysteries at Eleusis with the establishment of Dionysus Zagreus. Like Orpheus, Musaeus was originally from Pieria; with the Thracians he moved into Boeothia and was later at Athens.

G. Colli writes: 'The Parian Marble tells us that the person who established the Mysteries of Eleusis was Eumolpus, son of Musaeus. Various pieces of evidence confirm this, and others speak of a relationship between Musaeus and the Mysteries of Phlya.'[1]

During the same period (the 9th to 8th centuries B.C.) at ancient Thrace, in the North of Greece, there was a religious movement with a 'lunar' tendency and a mystical/evocative nature. Gradually, however, some of its 'Priestesses of the moon', or of the triple Hecate, took over the ancient worship of Bacchus and gave themselves up to degraded and unholy practices and thus gave rise to a bloodthirsty cult. These priestesses, who undertook these practices especially in the valley, in contrast to the Orphic

---

[1]   G. Colli, *La sapienza greca*, vol. I, Adelphi, Milan.

priests who would function on the mountains, took the name of Bacchantes, and their ritual celebrations became known as Bacchanals.

Lycurgus, son of Dryas and King of Thrace, sought to persecute them and stop their practices, going so far as to destroy the vineyards whose wine, which was now used in place of the original milk, was the source of harmful stimulation for the followers of Bacchus.

Into the religious scenario outlined so far and into this perverse Bacchic/orgiastic atmosphere of Thrace which humiliated masculine virility, stepped the inspired powerful figure of Orpheus, originating from the same country of Thrace.

He, who worshipped the Sun as an objective manifestation of the unmanifest solar Deity, went at night to the summit of Mount Pangaeus in order to be the first at dawn to pay homage to it and to chant the Hymn to Fire. It is worth noting that Pythagoras has it that the centre of the universe is Fire, of which the solar disc is but a reflection.

Unlike the Bacchantes, Orpheus followed the Solar Way, the Way of Fire; and a Fire was fed by the Orphic Priests as a living symbol of the spiritual Sun.

Orpheus – High Priest of Zeus and Apollo, lyre-player and singer, with the power to attract men and animals through the sound of his instrument – drew the great majority of the Thracians to himself, completely transformed the moon-worship of orgiastic Bacchus, and dispersed the Bacchantes, so that his influence spread as far as Greece. In this way he consecrated the sovereignty of Zeus in Thrace and that of Apollo in Delphi, where he laid the foundation of the law-court of the Amphictyonies which would later become the symbol for the social unity of Greece. He also introduced the Mysteries, raising the Bacchic/orgiastic Dionysus to the dignity of the

Mysteries of the heavenly Dionysus. From this it followed that Orpheus became the rectifier of Bacchic worship, the Pontiff of Thrace, the great Priest of Olympian Zeus and Hyperborean Apollo, and, for the Initiates, the one who established the Greater Mysteries.

> 'Blessed art thou, Callicles, for clearly you have been initiated into the Greater Mysteries before the Lesser Mysteries. And I believed that this could not be done.'[1]

As we may note, with Orpheus we rise to a metaphysical realm and a procedure that is genuinely initiatory.

Still with reference to Orpheus, Reale writes: 'The poet Ibycus, in the 6th century B.C., speaks of "the famous Orpheus", thereby giving witness to the great renown of this person at this time, which is explainable only through supposing the existence and spread of the religious movement related to him.

'Later Euripides and Plato give evidence in their own time to the great number of writings that were circulating under the name of Orpheus with regard to the Orphic rites and ceremonies of purification.

'Herodotus and Aristophanes also speak of Orphic rites and initiations. But perhaps most interesting of all is the evidence given by Aristotle, according to whom Onomacritus had set in verse teachings attributed to Orpheus. Now, since Onomacritus lived in the 6th century B.C., we have a firm and secure point of reference: in the 6th century B.C., verses were being composed under the name of the mythic poet, and so there existed a spiritual movement which acknowledged Orpheus as its patron and source of inspiration.'[2]

[1] Plato, *Gorgias*, 497 c.

[2] E. P. Lamanna, *Storia della filosofia antica*, vol. I, op. cit.

According to other witnesses, however, Orpheus can be traced back to a time prior to the Trojan War, and his life spanned several generations.

'Orpheus of Lebetra in Thrace, was the son of Oeagrus and Calliope. Oeagrus, for his part, was a fifth-generation descendant of Atlas, through Alcyone, a daughter of Atlas. Orpheus was born eleven generations before the War of Troy. They say that he was a disciple of Linus and that his life spanned nine (or, according to some, eleven) generations.'[1]

'Ellanic, Damaste, and Pherecides say that Homer was descended from Orpheus.'[2]

There are many disagreements about the birth and life of Orpheus, but it is also true that some 'figures' are able to walk among men, establish eternal truths, set up sacred institutions, and then disappear as if into a void, leaving nothing but mystery behind them. In other words, it means that there are some great Beings who have no personal history. One thing, however is certain: with Orpheus and Orphism the Western hemisphere took over the Greater and Lesser Mysteries, Mysteries which in time and space underwent adaptations and even theological superimpositions. The Christian Mysteries offer precise parallels with those of Orphism.[3]

Two 'myths/symbols' are linked to the person of Orpheus: his death at the hands of the Bacchantes, who tore his body to shreds, and his descent into the underworld (*katábasis*), which he undertook to bring his bride Eurydice back to life.

---

[1]   *I Presocratici. Testimonianze e frammenti*, vol. I. Laterza, Bari.

[2]   *Ibid.* vol. II.

[3]   See V. Macchioro, *Orfismo e Paolinismo.* Edizioni Bastogi, Foggia.

The first finds a counterpart in the death of Dionysus/ Zagreus, divine child and son of Zeus and Persephone, who was torn to shreds by the Titans but restored to life by Zeus. From the ashes of the Titans, who had been struck by the thunderbolt of Zeus, was born mankind, which thus bears within it both the divine essence absorbed from Dionysus/Zagreus and the earth element of the Titans.

Dionysus therefore dies, is restored to life, is exalted to Heaven, and is given the power to free man from the titanic element (see Plutarch, Diodorus, and others). Dionysus was also identified with Phanes, who in turn was identified with Zeus.

Phanes (Φανῆς) the hermaphrodite was born from the cosmic Egg, whose upper part became Heaven, while the lower part became Earth. The identification of Phanes with Zeus was represented by the swallowing of Phanes by Zeus (at the symbolic level).

Like all 'myths', this one does not represent a flight of fancy, but a *fact*, an *event*, which must be *actualised* by the candidate for initiation.

The 'myth' thus contains both the symbol and the *production* of an *experience*, because it is cathartic. If it does not become cathartic, it loses its function. The Dionysian Mystery, and therefore the Orphic Mystery, is a *fact*, not a theory: it is a precise experience which has to be actuated, but it is not an empirical experience or an experience of the sensible plane.

In Christianity, too, we find that Christ dies, is restored to life, exalted to Heaven, and given the power of redemption. Now the Passion of Jesus, His death, re-birth, and ascension are *facts* rather than theories: they must be lived, experienced, and realised by the Christian neophyte, if he truly wishes to follow and embody Jesus.[1]

Orpheus established the Mysteries, died (torn to pieces like Dionysus), returned to life, and holds the power of redemption/liberation. Dionysus/Zagreus is more than a historical event: it is supra-historical, an ever-present existing fact, a process which, if well conducted, produces real effects.

From this one can deduce that the mystical experience of the 'myth' involves a death (as far as the titanic element is concerned), a re-birth (to the Dionysian element), and hence an identity with the god. Only in this way is one regenerated in Dionysus, just as the Christian might say that he is regenerated in Christ.

On the other hand, it is also true that one can create an identity with the titanic element (even if this is not in absolute terms), so that there are titanic and satanic beings who can cause unlimited havoc.

It is to lead man back to the Divine, back to his true and blissful fold, that the initiatory Tradition, of which the Orphic Tradition is a legitimate Branch, helps us with its Teaching.

In metaphysical terms, the 'myth' of Dionysus represents the 'dismembering' of the One into the many.[2] The principial Unity differentiates itself, the Tree of Life is polarised into the Tree of Good and Evil (duality or the Pythagorean and Platonic dyad). This symbolism, however, is universal, and so we find in Egypt, for example, the death of Osiris through being torn to pieces.

---

[1]   See 'Initiation into the Mysteries of Love' in the Chapter 'Bhaktiyoga' of *Essence and Purpose of Yoga* by Raphael. Aurea Vidyā, New York.

[2]   See 'Hymn to Puruṣa', *Ṛg Veda* X, 90.

The second symbolism attributed to Orpheus is of a purely initiatory and practical order. The 'descent to the underworld' corresponds to the *nigredo* work of Alchemy[1]; Jesus, too, descends to the underworld, as must all who desire Realisation. Only in this way can the solar Fire shine within our purified, rectified, and pacified, consciousness.

Thus there are two symbols – one is universal, the other of an individual and practical operative order – which form part of the traditional Teaching. See the chapter 'The Orphic Ascesis' on page 95.

---

[1]   For the 'descent into the underworld', see 'Fire of Life', in *The Threefold Pathway of Fire* by Raphael, op. cit.

INNOVATIONS OF ORPHISM

As far back as some of the writings of the great Greek lyric poet Pindar, there appeared a vision of the world and man's destiny which was unknown to the Greeks and which may be considered quite extraordinary. A dominant aspect of this vision was one that would turn upside down the conception of culture and the very order of Greek society at that time. Until then, as we have seen, man was held to be mortal, and it was only by an heroic, Olympian deed, such as in battle, that he could win immortality and sit on the seat of the Gods. Immortality, therefore, was not offered to all, but to those few who, under the impulse of heroic deeds, could cross the abyss of the transience of the flesh.

With the new metaphysical Orphic vision, man was considered to be composed of an immortal part (Soul), which came from the divine, and a mortal part (body), which came from the titanic element. This immortal Soul could re-discover itself while the body was asleep, when it was quiescent during meditation/contemplation and at the death of the body itself. When the bonds which bound the Soul to the body were loosened, there was greater awareness of one's real immortal and divine nature.

Liberation from perishable mortality – which was essentially innate only in the gods and was granted exceptionally only to certain men capable of heroism – now became partially available to everyone and actually available to all who, on the way of awakening and with

proper stimulations (initiations) could have a real awareness of their own divine origin. This revolutionary conception, at least for the Greece of that time, took man
to a divine rank and raised him from a relative telluric
element to the grandeur of a god. Hence the birth of the
Sacred Mysteries, which maintained the identity of the
human Soul (the Dionysian part) with the divine nature,
the liberation of this Soul from the cycle of re-births, and
the ultimate Fullness of being.

In other words, Orphism led the Divine in man to
the transcendent Divine; and this is the task of the true
universal Mystery Tradition.[1]

Let us consider a few short extracts from Pindar,
Xenophon, and Aristotle, where these concepts are
expounded:

'And the bodies of all succumb to the power of
death.
But a living image of life abides, which alone comes
from the gods; and it sleeps
while the limbs are functioning;
but in the dreams of sleepers
it often shows the coming judgement of joys and
pains.'[2]

'For my part, my children, I have never succeeded in
convincing myself that the soul lives while it is in a
mortal body but dies when it is freed from it. In fact,
what I see is that the soul enlivens mortal bodies so
long as it resides within them. Again, I have never
convinced myself that the soul will be insensible once
it is separated from the body, which is insensible.

---

[1]   See Porphyry, *Life of Plotinus* 2, 25.

[2]   Pindar, *Odes and Fragments, fragment* 60.

Rather, when the spirit is separated from the body, then being pure and free from all admixture, it is logically more sensible than it was previously. When man's body dissolves, the individual parts are seen to rejoin the elements of their own nature, but not so the soul: it alone, present or absent, avoids being seen. Observe then, he continued, that none of the human conditions is closer to death than sleep is; and it is then that the human soul is better than ever at revealing clearly its divine nature; it is then that she doubtlessly foresees the future because she is freer than ever.'[1]

'Aristotle says that the idea of the gods has a double origin among men: what happens in the soul and heavenly phenomena. More precisely, what happens in the soul by virtue of the inspiration and prophetic power which are proper to it and which occur during sleep. In fact, when the soul in sleep recollects herself, then, assuming her true and proper nature, she prophesies and foretells the future. This is her condition when, at the moment of death, she separates herself from the body. And hence he gives his approval to the poet, Homer, for observing this, for he portrayed Patroclus, at the moment of being slain, as foretelling Hector's death, and Hector himself as foretelling Achilles' end. From facts such as these, he says, men suspected the existence of something divine within themselves, something similar to the soul and, more than all other things, the object of knowledge.'[2]

This is a vision which, as we have already noted, imparts to European civilisation an apparently new

---

[1]   Xenophon, *Cyropaedia*, VIII, 7, 21.

[2]   Ross, *On Philosophy, fragment* 12 a.

interpretation of human existence. We say 'apparently' because, in fact, the initiatory Teaching is supra-historical and therefore outside time.

Plato, too, speaks in similar terms in this passage from the *Cratylus*:

> 'In fact, some say that the body is the tomb [*sema*] of the soul, as if the soul were now buried; and since, on the other hand, it is through the body that the soul expresses all that it can express [*semainei*], this, too, is a reason for justly calling it a 'sign' [*sema*]. However, it seems to me that it was principally the followers of Orpheus that established this name, as if the soul were atoning for the faults that it has to atone for, and as if it had around it, to keep it in custody [*sozetai*], this enclosure which resembles a prison. This dungeon, then, as its name declares, is the custodian [*soma*] of the soul until it has paid all its dues, and there is nothing to change, not even a single letter.'[1]

The fact that the Orphists held that the Soul emanates from the Divine is also clear from the inscriptions of the *Golden Tablets* found in the tombs. On the tablet of Turi we read:

'I come pure from the pure, O Queen of the Underworld,
O Eucles and Eubuleus; and all you other immortal gods;
For I too glory in being of your divine race;
But I was cast down by Moira and the thunderbolt hurled from the stars.
I flew away from the painful arduous cycle,

---

[1]   Plato, *Cratylus*, 400 c.

With swift feet regained the longed-for crown,
And came down to the lap of the Queen, the lady of
the Underworld.
"Blessed and happy one, for from man you will be
a god."
You have fallen as a kid into the milk."[1]

The declaration that the Soul is of an order that is
supra-sensible is found in other *Tablets*, such as those of
Petelia and Pharsalus:

'I am the daughter of Earth and the star-spangled
Heaven.'[2]

This vision of the journey made by the being after
death revolutionised the cultural current of the day suf-
ficiently to overturn the conception of life, as Euripides
states in a significant passage:

'Who knows if living is not dying
And dying, in turn, is not living?'[3]

And in the *Gorgias* (492e) Plato makes sure that we
comprehend the truly revolutionary aspect of the message.
In fact, he goes so far as to formulate a new definition
of the whole of existence and, in particular, a mortifica-
tion of the body and of all that pertains to it, and a life
conformable to the Soul and what belongs to the Soul.

In some other *Golden Tablets* discovered in the tombs
of the Orphic members, we find affirmations of the divine
nature of the deceased Orphist, who has now transcended
the cycle of re-births, and we find indications about the

---

[1] *Tablet* of Turi, 1 (4th - 3rd century B.C.).

[2] *Tablet* of Pharsalus and Petelia (4th century B.C.).

[3] In *Heracles* 613 and *Cyclops* 646, 648, Euripides says that he has
had the privilege of seeing the magical rites of the initiates. This implies
that Euripides, in his turn, was initiated into the Orphic Mysteries.

journey which the Soul must undertake in the afterlife. This suggests that Orphism, like the Tradition in Egypt and Tibet[1], had a 'book of the dead' or at least some knowledge regarding the after-life, but this should not be surprising if one bears in mind, as has already been suggested, that Orphism has always belonged to the single universal Mystery Tradition.

'The undoubtedly great influence exerted by Orphism on the evolution of Greek spiritual life in general and of philosophy in particular comes from this accentuated internalisation of religious experience. Pythagoras and Plato drew from Orphism their conception of the body as a 'prison' or 'tomb' of the soul and also their view of metempsychosis as a necessary trial prior to final liberation from the cycle of births and deaths. The dualism of soul and body is the result of the rationalisation of the mythic antithesis between the Dionysian component and the titanic component within man. This is how, through Orphism, there entered into Greek culture the idea of an 'original sin', the idea of a life after death that was very different from the mere spectral survival of the Homeric tradition, the idea of the identification with the god as the final reward for the just, and the idea of the intrinsically corruptible nature of physicality.'[2]

And Colli goes even further, for he writes, 'With regard to Plato, then, it is possible, when he ventures to describe the cognitive experience of Ideas, to document the use of an Eleusinian terminology, so that one may posit the hypothesis that the theory of Ideas was originally an attempt in writing to divulge the Eleusinian

---

[1]   For a further enquiry, see the Chapter 'Post mortem and Bardo Thötröl' in *Beyond Doubt* by Raphael. Aurea Vidyā, New York.

[2]   *Dizionario di filosofia*. Rizzoli Editore, Milan.

Mysteries, forestalling the charge of impiety by avoiding
any reference to the mythic contents of Initiation.'[1]

And to support this proposal let us cite some passages in which Plato expresses himself in the language
of the Mysteries:

'As far as this level in the Mysteries of Love,
Socrates, you might perhaps have been able to initiate
yourself by yourself. But in the perfect and contemplative Teachings, to which – let us proceed properly
here – those that have been thus far expounded serve
as preparatory, I do not know whether you would
have the capacity. ... Inasmuch as someone who has
been trained so far in matters of Love by contemplating the Beautiful step by step and in the right way,
having reached the end of the Way of Love, will
on a sudden behold a Beauty of astounding nature:
precisely that Beauty, O Socrates, for which all the
earlier toils have been endured, that Beauty which in
the first place is eternal, which neither becomes nor
perishes, neither waxes nor wanes. ... Never again
in his eyes will Beauty assume the form of face or
hand or anything physical, or the form of speech or
knowledge ... but Beauty will appear to him as it is
in itself, ever the same as itself.'[2]

'But Beauty then shone in its fullness before our eyes
when, together with the chorus of the blessed – we
following Zeus, and others another god – we en-
joyed a sight and a spectacle that bestowed bliss and
we were initiated, it is proper to say, into the most
blessed of the Initiations which we celebrated, at the

---

[1] G. Colli, *La sapienza greca*, op. cit.

[2] Plato, *Symposium* 209 - 211 c.

time when, being perfected and immune to the evils that were waiting for us in the days to come, and being initiated into the most profound mysteries, we relished those visions that were perfect, simple, peaceful, and blissful, within a pure light, we ourselves being pure and not interred in this tomb which we call the body and which we drag about with us, being imprisoned within it like oysters in their shells."[1]

In these few lines Plato gives us to understand that:

1. Supreme knowledge is the fruit not of indirect mental discursiveness (διάνοια), but of direct noetic apprehension (νόησις). This means that Plato's philosophy is not mere philosophical sophistry (as it subsequently became for the most part, through the work of dianoetic philosophers), but a method conducive to *nóesis*.

2. He is acquainted with the Mystery-rites, from which it follows that he has received Initiation and that this Initiation was fully implemented, for he mentions 'perfect visions' and uses other phrases which concur with what *Vedānta* calls *samādhi*.

3. The words 'tomb', 'prison', and so on, with reference to the physical body, are exclusive to the Orphic vision.

4. The description of the Beautiful and of Initiation into the Beautiful gives us the intuition that he has been initiated into the Beautiful and has *seen* the Beautiful.

---

[1] Plato, *Phaedrus* 250 b-c.

Here is G. Colli once more: 'In Aristotle, who is certainly not the most mystical of philosophers, the topic is confirmed, and in quite explicit terms. In one passage we read that noetic knowledge is referred to the Eleusinian vision:

'... what belongs to teaching and what belongs to initiation. The former reaches men through hearing, while the latter does so when the *intuitive* faculty is *struck by a thunderbolt*, and this was called Mystery-related and resembled the Initiations at Eleusis.

'In fact, the sacred experience is not the domain of knowledge or a process of the mind ... the initiates are not obliged to apprehend [μαθεῖν] but to suffer [παθεῖν] and to put themselves into a particular disposition, as far, of course, as they are already predisposed to do so.'[1]

'And intuition of the intuitable, of the unadultered, and of the sacred – *flashing across the soul* like a thunderbolt – permitted touching and contemplation at a particular time and once only. This is why both Plato and Aristotle call this part of philosophy the supreme Initiation [*epoptéia*], insofar as those ... who have *directly touched* pure truth, with regard to that object, believe they possess the last word of philosophy, as in an Initiation.'[2]

'Moving from such a universal view,' Colli continues, 'I simply note here that the historical existence of the contemplative heights reached by what happened at Eleusis presupposes a religious setting which made it possible. Now it was precisely the god Dionysus who

---

[1]   Aristotle, *On Philosophy, fragment* 15.

[2]   Aristotle, *Eudemus*, fg. 10.

was behind Eleusis, who was worshipped at Eleusis, and who displayed his power at Eleusis.'[1]

Or rather, what is maintained is that Dionysus not only represented the Saviour of men but was also the founder of the Mysteries.

Indeed, Macchioro writes: 'Dionysus was not only the deity through whom the Mystery effected its redemptive work by identifying man with God, but he actually became the one who instituted the Mysteries, the one who bestowed this unique means of redemption.

'In the *Bacchantes* of Euripides, Dionysus says that he instituted the Mysteries in order to reveal himself to men as a god. Others who also attribute the Mysteries to Dionysus are Diodorus (III, 64, 7), Megastenes (38, 22), Strabo (X, 3, 10), the scholiasts of Homer (Schol. *Iliad*, VI, 131), Aristophanes (Schol. *The Frogs*, 343), Apollonius of Rhodes (Schol. *Apollonius of Rhodes*, II, 904) ...

This tradition which attributed the creation of the Mysteries to Dionysus acquired a special magnificence in the very long poem by Nonnus, which – through countless digressions and stories – is actually nothing but a glorification of Dionysus as the one who instituted the Mysteries ...

'No one will ever understand the religious development of Orphism without having clearly in mind the fundamental concept that for the Orphists their Religion (of the Mysteries) began with Dionysus, that it was through him that salvation came into the world, and it was through him that man found the way to reconcile himself with God.'[2]

---

[1]   G. Colli, *La sapienza greca*, op. cit. (Italics are ours).

[2]   V. Macchioro, *Orfismo e Paolinismo*, op. cit

And Orpheus represents the one who anchors to the earth the Mystery-Decree of Dionysus, the one who pursues the way of Dionysus to the point of creating identity with Dionysus.

> 'Blessed is the one who receives the grace
> to enter the divine Mysteries,
> sanctifies his life,
> consecrates his life in the thiasus,
> and piously purifies himself.'[1]

---

[1] Euripides, *Bacchantes* 72-77.

TRANSMIGRATION

There is no doubt that the idea of the transmigration of Souls – or of that part of the Soul that has 'fallen' and has been constrained by the titanic force – also has its origin in Orphism.

Zeller writes: 'In any case, it is clear that, among the Greeks, the doctrine of the transmigration of Souls did not reach the priests from the philosophers but came to the philosophers from the priests.'[1]

According to Reale, 'The following points should be noted: a) Pindar is acquainted with this belief, and it cannot be proved that he received it from the Pythagoreans rather than from the Orphists; b) again, when the ancient sources speak of transmigration, they refer to it as a teaching revealed by "theologians of old" and "priests", or they use expressions which they customarily apply to the Orphists; c) in the *Cratylus* Plato expressly refers to the Orphists, attributing to them the concept of the body as the place of expiation for the original sin of the soul, which structurally presupposes metempsychosis, and Aristotle, too, expressly attributes to the Orphists teachings which imply metempsychosis; d) some ancient sources clearly make Pythagoras depend on Orpheus, and not Orpheus on Pythagoras.'[2]

[1] Zeller-Mondolfo, *La filosofia dei Greci nel suo sviluppo storico*, I, 1. La Nuova Italia. Florence.

[2] E. P. Lamanna, *Storia della filosofia antica*, vol. I, op. cit.

Here are the fragments from Pindar:

'Of all from whom Persephone accepts
Deliverance from ancient punishment
She restores the souls to the sun shining on high
Through the turning of nine years.
They then arise as wondrous monarchs
And men of quick-acting might,
Sublime in wisdom; and mere mortals call them
Holy heroes for the times to come.'[1]

'Like the dead here, the guilty souls
At once pay off the penalty
And someone underground examines
The sins committed in this realm of Jove,
Proclaiming inexorable banishment,
And in ever-equal nights
And equal days the sun
Cheers the life of the just, free from all travail;
They do not make the earth quake
With the might of their arm,
Or the expanse of ocean for wretched food,
But revered among the gods
They joyfully keep the faith
And free from weeping pass their days;
While the evil-doers endure dreadful torments.
Yet he who dwells three times
In either of these realms
And keeps his soul from iniquity
Follows the way of Jove
Towards the tower of Chronos.
There, around the Isle of the Blessed,

---

[1]   Pindar, *fragment 68. Odes and Fragments*, op. cit.

Breezes blow from Ocean
And golden flowers flame.'[1]

With regard to Philolaus the Pythagorean, this is what Clement of Alexandria writes:

'The words of Philolaus are worth recording. The Pythagorean says, 'Even the *theologians* and *seers of old* bear witness that to expiate some sin the soul is united to the body and is as if buried in it.'[2]

In *Meno*, Plato writes, with reference to Pindar (*fragment* 127):

'Pindar, too, says the same, as do many other poets who have divine inspiration. And what they say is this ... They declare that the soul of man is immortal, and that there are times when it ends its earthly life – this is known as death – and there are times when it is reborn anew, but it never perishes: for these reasons we should live our lives in the holiest possible way.'[3]

In other places, when referring to the Orphic teaching, Plato often uses the expressions 'the ancient discourses', 'the ancient traditions', and 'the ancient sacred discourses'.

Aristotle, too, alludes to the 'theologians' and the 'ancients':

'There are some, then, who believe that even the most ancient theologians, of a generation far earlier than this ... And the poets of old consider this in a similar fashion.'[4]

---

[1] Pindar, *Olympian Odes*, 56-72.

[2] Clement of Alexandria, *Stromata*, III, 17 (Italics are ours).

[3] Plato, *Meno*, 81b-c.

[4] Aristotle, *Metaphysics*, 983b 27; 1091b 4.

'Which of us, thus, looking at all this, could think that we are happy and blessed? For no sooner are we born by the work of nature than we are doomed to suffer, as we are told by those who utter the Mystery-formulas. This is what those of the earliest antiquity say by divine inspiration, namely, that the soul pays a penalty and that we live in order to atone for grievous sins. In fact, the union of the soul with the body is clearly analogous to something of a similar nature: the Etruscans, we are told, often torture their prisoners by binding the living persons face to face with corpses, effecting an exact point of contact between the corresponding parts of the two bodies; and it seems that this is how the soul is arranged and united with all the physical parts of the body.'[1]

With regard to Pythagoras' dependence on Orpheus we quote this passage from Diogenes Laertius:

'Ion of Chios, in the *Triagmi*, attests that Pythagoras attributed some of his works to Orpheus.'[2]

Reale, too, writes: 'Fundamentally, transmigration has a moral meaning, which is very clearly indicated by Plato (apart from the well-known pages in the *Phaedo*) in two passages of the *Laws* (IX, 870 d-e; 872 e; 873 a), which it is appropriate to quote here:

"Let this be said by way of introduction to the treatment of this material, and let there be added to this the Tradition, to which many of those who in the initiations into the Mysteries are interested in these things give trust when they hear of it, that is, that in Hades there is punishment for such misdeeds, and

---

[1]　Aristotle, *Protrepticus, fragment* 10b. *Opere*, op. cit.

[2]　Diogenes Laertius, *Lives of the Philosophers*, VIII, 8.

that the perpetrators, after returning here once more, must of necessity pay the natural penalty, which is to suffer what they themselves have inflicted, thus ending their new life at the hands of others. This myth or Tradition, or whatever we should call it, clearly shows, therefore, as it has been transmitted to us from the priests of old, the fact that vigilant justice, avenger of the blood of relatives, follows the aforesaid law, and has for that reason established that anyone who commits an offence of this kind must necessarily suffer what he himself has inflicted: if he slays his own father, he must one day endure the same treatment at the hands of his children; and if he slays his mother, he must inevitably be born as a girl and later perish at the hands of the children; for there is no other expiation for family blood that has been criminally spilt, and the stain cannot be washed away unless the guilty soul has paid the price for slaughter, like for like, and has appeased the wrath of all the relatives."

'Among modern scholars it is Dodds[1] who most clearly expounds the meaning of these passages, for he writes: "Punishment in the after-life, however, failed to explain why the gods accept the existence of human suffering, and in particular the undeserved suffering of the innocent. On the other hand, re-incarnation explains it: with re-incarnation, there are no souls that are innocent, for all are atoning, at varying levels, for sins of varying gravity that have been committed in previous lives. And all this accumulation of suffering, in this world and the next, is but a part of the long education of the soul, which will

---

[1] E. Dodds, *The Greeks and the irrational.*

find its ultimate end in liberation from the cycle of re-births and the return of the soul to its divine origin".[1]

It needs to be clearly understood that these punish-ments and sufferings inflicted on the transmigrating soul are not meted out by a cynical, cruel God; nor, worse still, should they be understood to be vindictive acts per-formed by some supra-individual Divinity.

Nor is it a question of *lex talionis*, as some might think: Life, in its greatness, punishes no one and rewards no one: we punish ourselves and we reward ourselves, in accordance with the nature of the action, mental or physi-cal, which we perform. In other words, according to the biblical saying, 'whatsoever a man soweth, that shall he also reap'.[2]

The law of action and reaction is a natural *law*, like any other law at the level of manifestation.

If one dares to put a hand into the fire, of course one gets burnt and feels pain, but this painful occur-rence is something inflicted not by a capricious God, but by *ignorance* of a physical law. The universe is governed by laws, and breaking the law necessarily pro-vokes a response.[3]

Even the humblest innocent person, not knowing how a law operates, can encounter great suffering and serious conflicts.

Some might find it difficult to grasp this concept, which could be called scientific, because they are used to thinking of Divinity in terms of paternalism, oppor-

---

[1]   E. P. Lamanna, *Storia della filosofia antica*, vol. 1, op. cit.

[2]   St Matthew, 13:1-23; St Mark, 4: 1-20; St Luke, 8: 4-15; Hosea, 8: 7; *Galatians*, 6: 7-8.

[3]   See the Chapter '*Karma* or the law of cause and effect' in *The Pathway of Non-Duality*, by Raphael. Aurea Vidyā, New York.

tunism, emotion, personality, and even capriciousness, a Divinity that is ready to point the finger, sometimes to condemn and punish, sometimes to offer rewards and prizes. However, the law of action and reaction, like all the laws of the world of becoming, is not absolute, because it can be neutralised by another law, whose expression will have to reveal itself as equal and opposite. Thus hatred is neutralised by love, ignorance by knowledge, violence by comprehension and harmlessness, and so on.

The belief that nothing that is negative, painful, or conflicting can happen to a Saint simply because he is a Saint is a mistaken belief. It would be better to tell him if necessary, for example, not to touch high-tension electric wires, for he would be electrocuted, unless he knew a law whose application could neutralise the strong charge of the high-tension wires.

There is thus nothing unusual or improper about this law: if manifestation at the physical, subtle, and ethical (Ηθική) levels were not governed by laws, by Regulation/ Principle, we would have no science, no philosophy, no mathematics, no geometry, no impartial and invariable system of ethics, but instead we would have disorder, the whims of chance, unpredictability, utter individualism, and nothing but chaos.

'Like the birds, the wise look upwards: it seems to them that they are flying outside the body and towards a broad expanse of light, which bestows on their souls a sudden upward impulse far from all things mortal. And philosophy serves to prepare them for death. They consider the end of life to be an important blessing that is more than perfect because they believe that only then will the soul be able to live its real life, while at present the soul drowses and gathers nothing but the sort of impressions that are received from dreams."[1]

---

[1]   Plutarch, *That one cannot live happily following Epicurus.*

THE ULTIMATE DESTINATION OF THE SOUL

If, as we have seen, the Soul has 'fallen' to the plane of generation, if the body represents a limit, a prison which breaks the Soul's wings, if the world of dualistic experiences is nothing but a place of atonement (*karma*, according to *Vedānta*), then the final aim of the Soul must be to regain its freedom and its fullness.

If, in Homer's Greece, immortality and rewards and punishments were restricted to the very few people who displayed courage, passion, and Olympian strength, with the advent of Orphism everyone was able to re-discover his own immortality, and all were liable to receive rewards or punishments in accordance with their own actions. This meant that all beings had a *precise ethical responsibility*: to aim at overcoming the titanic element, a part of which they had each inherited.

Thus, with Orphism, man had an immediate imperative: to live in conformity with the universal or divine Law and consequently to re-discover his own supra-sensible origin. The two things are linked together. There is no other purpose on the plane of generation: everything else is merely *contingent activity*, which serves to keep us in life and perpetuate the titanic element.

This revolutionised the ethical and philosophical outlook of the Greeks and the Western world, because the *responsibility of one's own destiny* is given to the whole of humanity.

In the Homeric conception the many have no past and no future, because they have no present. With the Mystery-vision of Orphism man became an intelligible Soul, with a clear-cut responsibility and an immediate duty to *educate himself, know himself, and be.*

Pindar acts as the spokesman for this:

'For them the power of the sun shines forth,
While here below 'tis night;
Their seat is near the city, in the meadows of red roses,
With shady shrubs of incense <...>, and filled
<with trees> bearing golden fruit; and some disport
themselves with horses and bodily exercises, others with
games of chess, yet others with the sound of the lyre,
and in their midst abundance flourishes in full bloom:
a delightful fragrance wafts over that land,
as offerings of every kind are laid upon the altars of
the gods in the fire that can be seen from afar.'[1]

On the *Tablet* which has re-appeared at Petelia it says that the Soul will be with the other heroes. One of the *Tablets* at Turi states that just as the purified Soul was originally like the gods, so now it will be God and not a mortal being. This *Tablet* at Turi further declares that from a human being one will be reborn as God:

'But when the Soul abandons the light of the sun
Let it follow the path to the right ...
Rejoice, thou that hast undergone suffering...
which thou hast never previously experienced.
From man thou art born as God; as a kid,
thou hast fallen into the milk.
Rejoice, rejoice, as you take the path on the right

---

[1]   Pindar, *fragment* 129.

towards the sacred meadows and woods of Persephone.'[1]

With regard to the expression 'as a kid thou hast fallen into the milk' we quote some of the thoughts of Turchi, who sets it within the initiatory framework of Orphism.

'This expression does not signify the return of the soul (the kid) to the Milky Way, that is, to the heavens (Dieterich), or a ritual in which the initiate is immersed in a bath of milk (S. Reinach), or a mere proverbial saying meaning that the initiate is as pure as a sucking kid (Comparetti). Instead, in conformity with the mystical operations of initiation, it means that the initiate, by coming to resemble the divine kid which is Dionysus (who was in fact called ἔριφος in the so-called Orphic hymns), has also become a Dionysus himself, and that he has immersed himself in milk, food for the kid, being born anew, in the way that the Orphist, too, through initiation has plunged into a new divine life composed of that purity of which the white milk, nourishment for the newborn and for vegetarians, must have been, for the Orphists, the most obvious and appropriate symbol. It is equivalent to that other expression: "I, the new Dionysus, have attained divine life."

'This is confirmed by the fact that the expression immediately followed the firm declaration, "from man thou art become God", as if it were a clear expression of the transformation of a human being into the god, his deification by means of the mystical initiation.'[2]

---

[1] *Tablet* of Turi, 4 (4th-3rd centuries B.C.).

[2] N. Turchi, *Le religioni misteriosofiche del mondo antico.* I Dioscuri, Genoa

'From man thou art born a God', because, fundamentally, thou comest forth from the divine; indeed, for
Greece at that time, this was the most disconcerting nov-
elty conveyed by the new Mystery-Teaching.

How to escape from the cycle of re-births?

'To the left of the dwellings of Hades thou wilt find
a spring of water,
with a white cypress standing beside it:
do not approach this spring.
Thou wilt find another, with fresh clear water flowing
from the lake of Mnemosyne: before it guards are
stationed.
Thou wilt say, "I am the daughter of Earth and starry
Heavens,
and celestial is my race: this you also know.
I burn and I am dying of thirst. Now give me
straightway
of the fresh water which flows from the lake of
Mnemosyne."
They will allow thee to drink at the divine spring,
and from then on thou wilt reign with the other
heroes.'[1]

Turchi also writes, 'This burning thirst which consumes the soul is not physical ... it is the thirst for that
blissful immortality which is drawn from the spring of
Mnemosyne, the only possible refreshment for someone
who knows that he is a child of the starry heavens. And
the yearning to be re-united with the divine, from which
the soul has come, and the heart-ache, as it were, with
which it begs for the refreshing water of immortality, are

---

[1] *Tablet* of Petelia (4th century B.C.).

very effective proofs of the mystical heights to which Orphism was able to raise the faithful.'[1]

Colli writes, 'If one drinks of the stream of oblivion, one forgets everything but is born again to a new life, that is, the thirst is merely deceived and it is not long before it re-appears in a new individuality. But if one drinks from the spring of Mnemosyne, then, as these Tablets bear witness, memory revives the knowledge of the past and of the unchangeable, and the man acknowledges his divine origin and identifies himself with Dionysus; and the burning thirst is not extinguished but is quenched by an ice-cold, divine knowledge which gushes forth. Life is not negated and not even replaced by another burning thirst, but is overwhelmed by a different life, the Dionysiac life.'[2]

Oblivion/λήθη refers to the state of ignorance after the fall of the soul into the body, and the absence of oblivion (ἀλήθεια = truth) refers to that state in which Knowledge is realised.

Plato takes up this concept of *forgetting* and *remembering* or *waking up,* to postulate knowledge which is *a priori* or innate in the Soul.

And Proclus, referring to Plato, bears witness to these two states in the following words:

'To oblivion (λήθη) and to the remembrance of eternal discourses (ἀίδιοι λόγοι) philosophy attributes, respectively, the cause of our estrangement from the gods and our return to them.'[3]

[1] N. Turchi, *Le religioni misteriosofiche del mondo antico*, op. cit.

[2] G. Colli, *La sapienza greca*, op. cit.

[3] Proclus, *Chaldean Philosophy*, 5. cit.

As we have shown in *Initiation into the Philosophy of Plato*, *Vedānta* also follows this metaphysical vision.[1] In the *Bhagavadgītā* (XVIII, 73), towards the end of the philosophical dialogue on realisation between Arjuna and Kṛṣṇa, Arjuna declares, 'I have regained my memory.' He has finally woken up from the long 'veiling sleep' and has re-discovered his memory, which has been clouded over by *avidyā*/ignorance. Rather than 'ignorance', which is the usual translation of this word, *avidyā* indicates that condition on account of which there is forgetting, oblivion, not knowing oneself as undivided Unity, which would be Platonic 'reminiscence'.

This shows that Orphism is a traditional Teaching with a place in that line of transmission which links the various traditional Branches.[2]

---

[1] See the Chapter 'Platonism and *Vedānta*' in *Initiation into the Philosophy of Plato*, by Raphael, op. cit.

[2] For a deeper understanding, see *Initiation into the Philosophy of Plato*, op. cit.; *Brahmasūtra* by Bādarāyaṇa, edited by Raphael, op. cit.

THEOGONY

In his introduction to the *Orphic Hymns*, Giuseppe Faggin notes that 'apart from the Theogony of Hesiod and those attributed to Musaeus, Acusilaus, Pherecydes, and Epimonides, there are three Orphic theogonies; the one which is "of very great antiquity" and of which we have the Aristotelian/Eudemean version, together with the version preserved for us by Apollonius of Rhodes; the Theogony known as "Hieronymian" because it was expounded by a certain Hieronymus who goes back to the logographer Hellanicus of Lesbos (this has been preserved for us by Damascius, Apion, and Athenagoras); and lastly, that Theogony which is called "rhapsodic" and is composed of an indefinite number of ἱεροὶ λόγοι arranged (in conformity with the number of cantos found in Homer) is twenty-four rhapsodies, of which we have several fragments; from the time of Syrianus this Theogony had great significance for the Neoplatonists because it contained the myth of Dionysus/Zagreus, in which it was easy to rediscover the symbols which were most akin to their own metaphysics and mysticism.'[1]

'Now in these Orphic rhapsodies of the Tradition the following Theogony ... was also explained by those philosophers who put Time in the place of the single principle of all things, Ether and Chaos in the place of the two principles, refer to the Egg instead of that which is the all, and present this as the first triad. And they compose the second triad of the created Egg and

---

[1] Cp., *Inni Orfici*, Edited by G. Faggin.

that which bears the god within itself, or the resplen-
dent tunic, or even the cloud, for it is from this that
Phanes leaps forth ... The third triad is then formed of
Metis (understood as intuition), Erychepeus (understood
as power), and Phanes himself (understood as Father)
... This, in truth, is the customary Orphic theology.'[1]

'In the beginning Ether, created by God, revealed itself
to Time; and on both sides of Ether there was Chaos;
and dark Night covered all things and concealed what
was beneath the Ether ... And Orpheus said that the
Earth was invisible on account of the Darkness ...
saying that the Light which had split the Ether was
that being ... which was higher than all and whose
name Orpheus himself, after hearing it from the oracle,
revealed as Metis, Phanes, Erychepeus.'[2]

'According to Orpheus, four reigns were transmitted:
the first was the reign of Uranus, who was succeeded
by Chronos ... after Chronos Zeus ruled ...later
Dionysus succeeded Zeus.'[3]

'You must therefore think of Chronos as Time and
of Rhea as the flow of moist substance, for all of the
matter conveyed by time begat, in the form of an Egg,
the spherical Sky which enfolds everything ... In fact,
from inside the surface of the sphere a Creature, both
male and female, was formed from a matrix through
the foresight of the divine Breath contained within
it, and Orpheus calls this Phanes, because when it
appeared to him the whole shone through its work,

---

[1]   Damascius, *On First Principles.*

[2]   G. Malalas, *Cronografia,* 4, 89.

[3]   Olympiodorus, *Commentary on the Phaedo of Plato,* 61 c.

through the effulgence of the most splendid of the elements: the fire which reaches perfection in moisture.'[1]

The Orphic Theogony is not a parody of Hesiod's, as Rohde rightly notes: 'Keeping clearly to that very ancient Greek Theogony, which had been gathered together within Hesiod's poem, these Orphic Theogonies described the coming into being and development of the world from dark primitive impulses up to the clearly defined multiplicity of the cosmos based on unity; and they described it as the history of a long series of Powers and divine Beings which, developing one from another, with one overcoming the other, alternated in the work of forming and ruling the world, absorbing it all into themselves before restoring it as something enlivened by a single breath and as One in its limitless plurality.'[2]

According to Guthrie, the Orphic Theogony ends with the myth of Dionysus and the Titans, thus endowing the human being with a dual origin which is also an ethical one. This implies, in contrast to Hesiod's Theogony, that the Orphic vision could constitute a true *religio*, with a specific experience of spiritual life.

From this Plato derives the vision of being into the intelligible and the sensible, inasmuch as these two dimensions are not opposed to each other.[3]

Of the Theogonies which are attributed to Orphism, let us review the one based on the indications given by Plato, Aristotle, and Eudemus of Rhodes (see the diagram on page 79), by making just a reference to the so-

---

[1]   Apion, in Clement of Alexandria, *Roman Homili* 6, 5.

[2]   E. Rohde, *Psyche: the cult of the souls and belief in immortality among the Greeks.*

[3]   On this subject see the Chapter 'Platonic dualism?' in *Initiation into the Philosophy of Plato,* op. cit.

called Rhapsodic Theogony, since there are no substantial differences.

> 'To Know and expound the origin of the other gods is an undertaking that is beyond our powers, and we should trust those who have spoken of this in earlier times, for being, as they declared, descendants of the gods, they should, I believe, have been well acquainted with their forebears ... So, as far as we are concerned, let the birth of these divinities be as they report it, and let it be proclaimed so. From Gaia and Uranus were born Tethys and Ocean, and from these two were born Rhea and Chronos and all those who accompanied them; and from Chronos and Rhea were born Zeus and Hera.'[1]

All these names, of course, are personifications of principles. The deities themselves are objectivisations of universal Essences; and insofar as this is a traditional Theogony it is linked, with various modifications, to the other Theogonies.

Night represents the Unbegotten, Non-Being, the unqualified Absolute; it is the metaphysical Zero, or the metaphysical One, which transcends manifestation although it is its foundation. It corresponds to the One-One, or Supreme, of Platonism, to the *nirguṇa Brahman* of *Vedānta*, to the *Tem* of the initiatory Teaching of Egypt, and to the *Ain Soph* of *Qabbālāh*:

> 'Night in Orpheus is the same as *Ain Soph* in *Qabbālāh*.'[2]

Gaia and Uranus represent the first metaphysical, polar dyad, the intelligible 'essence' and 'substance' of

---

[1]   Plato, *Timaeus*, 40, d-e.

[2]   G. Pico della Mirandola, *Conclusiones orphicae*, X, 15.

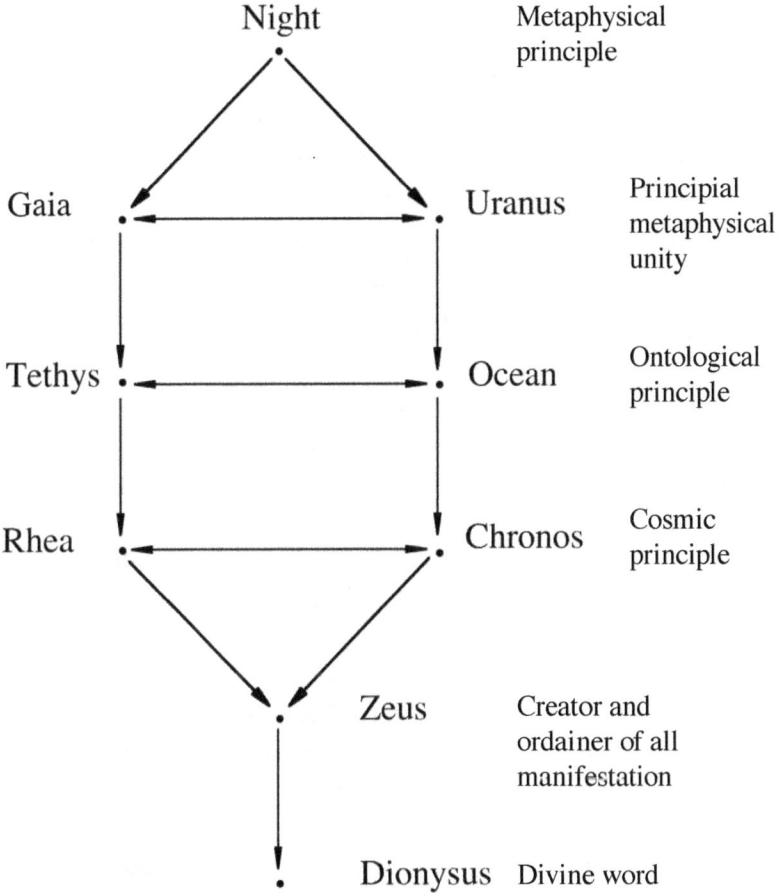

divine order, prior to objective manifestation. It is a polar unity which contains all the potentialities of manifestation.

Ocean represents the supernal, universal waters, the Abyss which is ready to manifest the golden Egg that contains the entire objective world. It defines the limits of the creation; the whole emerges from the Waters, and the Whole returns into the unfathomable Abyss.

Chronos in his polar aspect represents the manifested cosmic Egg; it is the golden Egg (*Hiraṇyagarbha*) of the *Vedānta* Tradition. It is also the great Time which encompasses the flow of becoming.

'You must therefore think of Chronos as Time, and of Rhea as the flow of moist substance.'[1]

The flow of formal becoming is contained within the great Time which, together with Necessity, winds around the universe like a snake.

According to G. de Santillana, Plato 'is quoting an Orphic version (hence his reluctance to name his authoritative sources), and the strange beings which appear there, such as Ocean and Chronos, merit our attention. What is meant here is not Chronos as Saturn, but Chronos as Time.'[2]

According to Onians, Okeanos is being compared to Achelous, the primordial river which 'was represented as a snake with horns and a human head ... The procreative element in the body was the ψυχή which manifested in the form of a snake. It is now clear that Ὠκεανός was the ψυχή of the beginnings, for this reason conceived as a snake, connected to the fluid of procreation ... Thus according to Homer, who through allusions is referring

---

[1]   Apion, in G. Colli, *La sapienza greca*, op. cit.

[2]   G. de Santillana, *Hamlet's Mill*.

to the conception shared by his contemporaries, the universe was shaped like an egg surrounded by Ὠκεανός, which is the generation of everything ... Moreover, one will have a better understanding because in this Orphic vision [*fragments* 54, 57-58 Kern] the snake was called Χρόνος and because, to someone who asked what Χρόνος was, Pythagoras replied that it was the soul of the universe ... According to Pherecydes, from the seed of Χρόνος were produced fire, air, and water.'[1]

And de Santillana also says, 'The great Orphic entity was Cronus Aion (the Zend-Avesta *Zurvan akarana*), generally understood as 'endless Time' .... It is well known that for the Orphists Chronos was the *paredrus*[2] of Ananke, Necessity, which according to the Pythagoreans, also surrounds the universe. Time and Necessity which surround the universe: here is a concept that is quite clear and fundamental; it is linked to the movements of the heavens, regardless of biology, and it leads directly to the Platonic idea of time as "a moving image of eternity" [Plato, *Timaeus*, 37d].'[3]

According to the rhapsodic Theogony, from the Cosmic Egg was born Phanes, who was assimilated into Eros, Metis, Erychepeus.

Sabbatucci writes: 'The real quality of Eros, which measures his stature, appears in the *Symposium* as the capacity to integrate and reconcile opposites ...

'In fact, Eros is excluded from the system which is expressed poetically by Hesiod; the system needed the Orphic Revolution for the god to become Protogonos/Phanes ...

---

[1] R. B. Onians, *The Origins of European Thought.*

[2] A word used in Greek religion to refer to a deity associated in worship with a greater deity.

[3] G. de Santillana, *Hamlet's Mill.*

Now, from that short period of time in Greek civilisation which Plato picks up and presents in his *Symposium* ... we are able to extract the elements which will explain to us what happened to Eros in the Orphic setting. In the Greek cosmos of Hesiod, the god is the integrator/unifier who has his *raison d'être* as "order" only in a universe which has been shattered and partitioned out in countless finite and limited forms. Even the negative, or Orphic, verdict about the cosmic partitioning is clear from the pages of the *Symposium* ...

'The Eros who joins, that is to say, who "mystically" unites, is the very antithesis of the principle which moves the Theogony of Hesiod, where everything takes form by separating itself, detaching itself, and distinguishing itself from the original "unformed" and "imperfect" condition.'[1]

For Hesiod, the fragmentation, the differentiation of forms - that is to say, multiplicity - represents perfection; for Orpheus, by contrast, it is the source of degradation, imperfection, and alienation from the primordial Unity.

In the Orphic Theogony, Eros represents 'that happy, but lost, pre-cosmic moment when all was the All, offering the image/model of a "regainable" state of bliss.'[2]

The separation, differentiation, and 'rending' of the universal Unity are the effect of *Neikos* (νεῖκος = contention/opposition), while the solution[3] of separative polar duality is effected by Eros.

According to Orphism, Phanes/Eros is assimilated into Dionysus as the means which unifies and merges duality

---

[1]   D. Sabbatucci, *Saggio sul misticismo greco.* Ateneo, Rome.

[2]   *Ibid.*

[3]   Solution: 1. the action or process of solving; the state, condition, or fact of being solved. To Solve: 4. to dissolve, put an end to... 5. to dissolve, to melt.

into unity. In Christianity, too, Christ is the one who unites the fallen creature to the Creator:

'No man cometh unto the Father, but by me.'[1]

The Platonic conception of Eros is particularly Orphic, just as the Neikos/Eros of Empedocles is Orphic, with the same four basic elements of Empedocles, and just as the function of Dike/Eros is also Orphic in the Poem of Parmenides.

From the polarity of Chronos and Rhea is born Zeus, who is the King and Lord of the world; he is father and mother of all manifest beings; he is 'the one who assigns a place to each and every thing, the ordainer of the entire cosmos.'[2]

'And the poets of old think likewise, for they say that rule and lordship are not given to the primordial deities such as Night, Heaven, Chaos, or Ocean, but to Zeus.'[3]

Dionysus represents the Logos, the solar Word, the Saviour of humanity. He corresponds to *Viṣṇu* of *Vedānta*, to the Persian Mithras and the Egyptian Horus. Orpheus is the one who anchors the Logos to the earth, the one who, by transmitting the sacred Mysteries of Dionysus, makes redemption and liberation possible for men, bound as they are to the titanic element.

The Christian theological trio of God, Christ, and Jesus is analogous to the Mysteries of Dionysus. Zeus offers his son, Dionysus, as the regenerative divine Word, incarnated in Orpheus, the visible instrument of liberation.

Again, in the *Corpus Hermeticum* of Hermes, the thrice-greatest, we find:

---

[1]   St John, 14: 6.

[2]   Damascius, *On First Principles*, 123 bis, op. cit.

[3]   Aristotle, Metaphysics N 4, 1091 b, 46.

'This light am I, Intelligence [the *Noûs* of the Greek Tradition], your God, who am before the moist nature emanating from Darkness; and the Word of light proceeding from Intelligence is the Son of God.'[1]

This is related to the Gospel of St John:

'In the beginning was the Word, and the Word was with God, and the Word was God.'[2]

And again in the Corpus Hermeticum:

'The Word of God rose at once from the lower elements into the pure creation of nature and became one with Thought the creator.'[3]

And in St John:

'All things were made by him [the Word]; and without him was not any thing made that was made.'[4]

Through the Sacred Mysteries of Orpheus one attains identity with Dionysus and consequently with all the Principles which stand behind him. The titanic element breaks the link with the Divine; the Dionysian element re-establishes it. According to the Orphists, Dionysus is still the ruler of the present age. Adding a geometrical representation of the Orphic Theogony might make it easier for the reader to understand (see the diagram on page 85).

In another Theogony, the one contained in the Orphic Rhapsodies, Chaos and Ether are also spoken of. The term 'Chaos' is also known to us: it is the immensity of primordial space; and it is everything that becomes, appears, and disappears within this space; it also represents

---

[1] Hermes Trismegistus, *Pimander*, I, 6. (Square brakets are ours).

[2] St John, I: 1.

[3] Hermes Trismegistus, *Pimander*, I, 10, op. cit.

[4] St John, I: 3.

•   Metaphysical Principle or first
      determination of the unbegotten
      Night

•⟵————————⟶• The principial Point doubles, and
              polarity/dyad, in its potential
              state, manifests itself

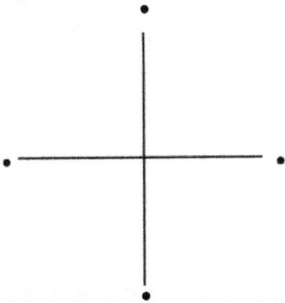

Great Time and Space are born

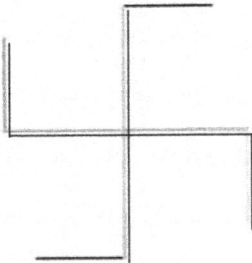

Zeus sets the cosmic process in
motion by offering Dionysus as the
redeeming Word for fallen beings

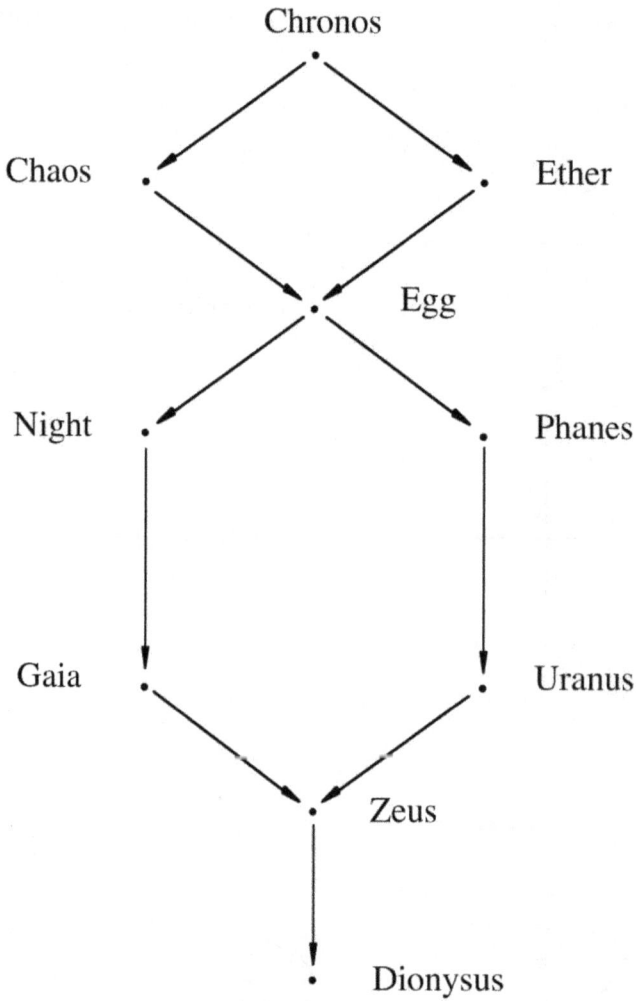

the unfathomable Waters before they appear as form and name. But the manifestations which appear within Chaos are Cosmos. Cosmos is therefore the world of names and forms, all that is born or manifests from Chaos under the impulse of Ether (universal Spirit), the other polarity.

Although we may change some names and reverse others, the result is always the same. Here is how this Theogony unfolds (see the diagram on page 86).

Here Chronos is positioned as the origin of everything, but the essence which gives form to this Principle does not change.

Ether and Chaos constitute the dyad from which emerges the cosmic Egg which contains everything. They are the totality of the cosmos waiting to be split open and therefore made manifest. Phanes and Night are the two primordial principles which have come forth from the cosmic Egg and which can be related to *essence* and *substance*. In Gaia and Uranus they become objective manifestation, revealing themselves as Earth and Heaven, or the sensible and the intelligible.

ORDER / UNIVERSAL HARMONY

'Orphic Mysticism and philosophical speculation (which distinguished itself from religion by going beyond the prevailing polytheism and was therefore able to take its place on the same level as mysticism in antithesis to the polytheistic system) sometimes agreed with each other in formulating an absolute principle which transcended (or was higher than) the gods themselves and which justified and gave meaning to the multiform manifestations of the world of becoming, manifestations which undermined the authenticity of a static reality that was effectively represented by the immortal gods.'[1]

In contrast to the individual and collective unpredictability of the gods and men of the Homeric tradition, Orphism posits in Adrasteia a principle of universal law and harmony which stands not only above men but also above the gods. Adrasteia, in fact, represents this principle of Law, Order, and Norm which pervades the whole of manifestation. It corresponds to the Principle of *Manu*, the lawgiver of the *Vedānta* tradition. This is the principle which is taken up later by various philosophical currents under different names: Ananke, Dike, Nemesis, Themis, and so on.[2]

This implies that manifestation is not governed by the unpredictability of its manifold movements, or by whimsical and exclusive chance, but by Law, that Law which refers

---

[1] D. Sabbatucci, *Saggio sul misticismo greco*, op. cit.

[2] Cf. Parmenides, *On the Order of Nature*, op. cit.

multiplicity itself to unity. It corresponds to *Dharma*, or conformity to the universal Principle, and consequently to the Law of Harmony which this Principle ordains and which flows forth from this principle.

According to *Vedānta*, *Dharma* represents that through which Harmony manifests as an expression of the Unity of Being.[1]

Science, philosophy, art itself, and so on, can exist only because, behind the changes of form, there is a constant, a common denominator towards which all appearances are directed and which offers the certainty of an ordered sequence of events and things.

'If nothing eternal existed, even becoming would be impossible.'[2]

Man is not the result of chance or accident: he is the immortal Being which becomes part of the great scheme of supreme reality (Gaia and Uranus).

In place of the indeterminate nature of form, in place of titanic substance, Orphism posits a reality which is universal, noumenal, and teleological, because although being can conceive itself as becoming and process, it cannot, sooner or later, be anything but Being.

'From being man, you have realised yourself as God', and this can be said to be a possibility because man has always been a god. Manifestation and the expression of being tend, consciously or unconsciously, towards an end which is that of rediscovering and recognising what one really is. And in this process of recognition one is helped

[1]   For a deeper understanding of *Dharma*, in conformity to the universal Principle, see 'Universal Order (*Ṛta*)' in Preface, and especially 'Reflections on Chapter Four', in *Bhagavadgītā*, edited by Raphael. Aurea Vidyā, New York.

[2]   Aristotle, *Metaphysics*, B, 4, 999 b 5.

by a universal reality whose characteristic is not *chaos* but *cosmos*, as personified by Adrasteia. Adrasteia represents the measure/order which is inherent in the cosmic Egg, and when Adrasteia reveals itself, the subtle and gross manifestation receives order and measure.

'And so it is written, "The first man Adam was made a living soul"; the last Adam was made a quickening spirit. How be it that was not first which is spiritual, but that which is natural; and afterward that which is spiritual.

'The first man is of the earth, earthy: the second man is the Lord from heaven. As is the earthy, such are they also that are earthy: and as is the heavenly, such are they also that are heavenly. And as we have borne the image of the earthy, we shall also bear the image of the heavenly. Now this I say, brethren, that flesh and blood cannot inherit the kingdom of God; neither doth corruption inherit incorruption ...

'So when this corruptible shall have put on incorruption, and this mortal shall have put on immortality, then shall be brought to pass this saying that is written, Death is swallowed up in victory. O death, where is thy victory? O grave, where is thy sting?'.

'For we know that if our earthly house of this tabernacle were dissolved, we have a building of God, an house not made with hands, eternal in the heavens. For in this we *groan*, earnestly desiring to be clothed upon with our *house* which is from *heaven*. For we that are in this tabernacle do groan, being burdened: not for that we would be unclothed, but clothed upon, that mortality might be swallowed up of life ... Therefore we are always confident, knowing that, whilst we are at home in the body, we are absent from the Lord: (for we walk by faith, not by sight) we are confident, I say, and willing rather to be absent from the body, and to be present with the Lord.'[1]

We should note that Hermes Trismegistus, too, in showing his son Tat the way that leads to new birth, calls the body a 'tabernacle' (σκῆνος):

> 'This tabernacle that we have crossed, my son, is made by the zodiacal circle ... According to the hymn of praise revealed by Pimander, you are hastening with good reason, my son, to escape from your tabernacle (from your body) because you are purified.'[2]

The indications both of Saint Paul and of Hermes correspond to the Orphic teaching.

---

[1] St Paul, I *Corinthians* 15: 45, 54-5; II *Corinthians* 5: 1-8. (Italics are ours). This letter from St Paul could also have been written by a follower of Orphism: there would be no discordance.

[2] Hermes Trismegistus, *Pimander*, XIII, 12, 15, op. cit.

THE ORPHIC ASCESIS

Orphism does not emphasise just the cosmogonical aspect and the state of the gods as universal principles, but, unlike the vision of Hesiod, it also turns its attention to man as he is, by defining him and endeavouring to exalt him to his true divine dignity. Hence the birth of the Mystery Initiation.

Sabbatucci writes: 'Hesiod circumscribes the human condition within a very limited part of his universe, and he limits himself to teaching man how the universe itself was made, the human rôle and the divine rôle, and consequently the norms that man must keep for a 'correct' way of behaving .... It will not be like this for the Orphists, who will be interested in anthropogony as much as in Theogony.'[1]

So, like all traditional Teachings, Orphism goes back to the 'fall' of one part – a 'reflection' or ray of light, or a 'fragment' of the Soul – into the world of generation and corruption (as Saint Paul puts it) or the titanic world. In other words, the human being, as such, has a part which is divine, Dionysian, and immortal and which belongs to the realm of the intelligible; and the human being also has a 'fragment' which has fallen into the physical body and which interacts with the sphere of the sensible, the sphere composed of bodies and forms that are subject to corruption. The Soul, or *psyché*, is the intermediary between the Dionysian intelligible and the titanic sensible or the *soma* (σῶμα)/body which is completely sensible.

---

[1]   D. Sabbatucci, *Saggio sul misticismo greco*, op. cit.

The *psyché* struggles between *Noûs*, its divine counterpart, which attracts it, and the body/*soma*, which holds it back.

So we may say, with Orphism, that the fallen 'fragment' has made a 'tomb' (σῆμα) for itself, a prison, being now constrained by the laws of necessity and the laws of becoming. This is the 'Tomb of Osiris' in the Hermetic tradition. From this comes the transmigration of this 'fragment' of consciousness which remains operative until this embodied reflection of consciousness is re-integrated within the Soul to restore Unity.

If we bear in mind that Orphism, like the other Traditions, considers the Soul to be immortal, we can deduce from this that the Soul is outside time, space, and causality. Now for anyone who possesses this incorporeal and intelligible nature, to plunge into the realm of the sensible and corruptible, even with just one of his extensive rays, means finding himself in a 'tomb', a prison. These are images denoting constriction and reduction of capacity, ability, and possibility.

If anyone thinks that Orphism conceives of the corruptible in ultra-pessimistic terms (then see Plato himself and Saint Paul), we should bear these presuppositions in mind. A limit for the absolutely Limitless cannot but represent a 'prison', a true 'tomb'. According to Orphism, the plane of sensible generation is σῶμα-σῆμα, an abnormal plane, *sui generis*, a plane of sheer, accidental, headlong falling, a plane which there might never have been, a plane which draws its nourishment from self-ignorance (the *avidyā* of *Vedānta*).

The normal, genuine homeland of true and immortal being is not this dualistic world, it is another world, one made of bliss. 'Our homeland is that from which we come, and up yonder is our Father.'[1]

As a state of consciousness, it is a world which is not born and does not die, while this world is born and has to die. Or rather, we need to acknowledge that all compounds, and therefore all bodies, on the sensible plane move inexorably towards their own dissolution, towards the simple and the elementary. To hold a body together requires force, as the intrinsic nature of the elements tries to regain its freedom. All the component parts of things must vanish. Every datum, whatever its origin and constitution, holds within itself the implicit necessity to dissolve. Every phenomenal or sensible substance is merely a continuity of changes, each of which is determined by its pre-existing conditions. A datum is just a force, an effect, a condition which appears and disappears.

The Soul, being attached to its fragment, is thus a prisoner of this incessant becoming, so that it seeks its release into freedom.

Hermes Trismegistus says to his son, Tat:

'My son, it is impossible to be attached at the same time to the mortal and to the divine. Beings are of two kinds: corporeal and incorporeal; and in them the mortal and the divine are distinct. The choice of one or the other is left to the will. For one cannot be attached to both at once. When the choice has been made, the one that is abandoned reveals the power of the other. And choosing the better is not only excellent for the chooser, *making the man God* ...'[2]

---

[1]   Plotinus, *Enneads*, I, VI, 8.

[2]   Hermes Trismegistus, *Pimander*, IV, 6-7, op. cit. (Italics are ours).

According to the Gospels, 'No man can serve two masters' (St Matthew, 6:24) and 'No man putteth new wine into old bottles' (St Luke, 5:37).

According to Aristotle, identity must permeate every change; all changes imply something permanent which represents the cause of change itself.[1] According to Kant, no temporal relationship is possible without the permanent;[2] without the constant, no temporal relationships can originate.

It is not possible to consider reality as a mere network of relationships and connections without something to connect and relate to. If every sensible datum finds its sufficient cause in another datum, which in turn finds its cause in yet another datum, and so on *ad infinitum*, then on the basis of this hypothesis it is certainly impossible to find the true cause of every datum. From this it follows that we must go beyond the category of cause and effect, until we reach a datum which is *causa sui*, which is ipseity and not abaliety[3], and which therefore remains identical to itself by transcending all possible changes.

Sensible existence is change, and change does not bring *stable* knowledge or *summa pax*.

From this perspective, we can agree with Sophocles when he states, under Orphic inspiration:

'Not to be born! This is what transcends all thought. But if someone appears in the world of existence, there is something else that is meaningful: returning as quickly as possible whence one has come.'[4]

And the words of Pindar say no less:

---

[1] Cf. Aristotle, *Physics*, VII, 242, lines 1-35; *Metaphysics*, II, 2, 994 b, lines 1-5.

[2] Kant, *Critique of Pure Reason*. First Analogy of Experience.

[3] Abaliety: quality of a datum which has its cause in another datum.

[4] Sophocles, *Oedipus at Colonus*, 1225-7.

'Ephemeral beings! What is each of us? Man is a dream of a shadow.'[1]

If we have plunged into non-being by 'accident' or through free choice, our duty and destiny is to 'restore wings to the Soul', that it may fly without delay towards its natural homeland.

In *Initiation into the Philosophy of Plato* we wrote: 'The "flight" from the body and from the world is certainly a flight, but not towards annihilation and avoidance. Rather it is a flight towards the true Homeland of Being, a flight from the world of shadows, from the sensory/emotional/irrational ... It is not a flight from physical or psychological pain, not a flight from individual contingent responsibilities, but it is something more: it is the flight of the Philosopher who, through pure contemplation, has embraced the inadequacy, the transitoriness, the emptiness, the inconsistency, the insubstantiality of the sphere of the material and sensible. We may say more: the Philosopher's flight is not a flight, for from what does he have to flee if things are not?'[2] Hence the Orphic Ascesis of the Soul, the way of return, the way of conversion, of internalisation, and of 'remembering'.

Colli writes: 'To have exalted memory in this way – for it is only by looking back that time exalts – is a decisive metaphysical sign: and not only for the pessimistic and anti-historical consequence, but above all for the indication of an absolute place – which is the beginning of time – that is detached from all other experiences. Now, it is precisely this detached beginning which can be grasped anew during our life if we *manage to break*

---

[1] Pindar, *Pythian Odes*, VIII, 95-97.

[2] See Chapter 'Platonism and *Vedānta*' in *Initiation into the Philosophy of Plato*, op. cit.

the individuality. It is Mnemosyne which enables us to do this. In this way, the transcendence of Orpheus is also immanence, and his pessimism is *also optimism*, if we follow the inspiration of Dionysus."[1]

The Orphic ascesis, to 'break the individuality', is offered in four stages to those who are being initiated:

1. Purification
2. Descent to the underworld (*katábasis*)
3. Becoming unified with one's own Daimon/Soul
4. Identity with the celestial Dionysus.

We saw earlier that one of the 'myths' of Orpheus is that of the 'descent to the underworld'.

Now those who have an inside appreciation of initiatory matters are able to understand this particular symbolism. In fact, it belongs to all the initiatory Traditions, such as those of Sumeria, Babylon, and Assyria. So there is the 'descent to the underworld' of Ishtar, the female divinity of the Babylonian and Assyrian pantheon; the 'descent to the underworld' of Inanna, the Sumerian goddess of mother earth; the 'descent to the underworld' of Jesus Himself; and so on.

Moreover, this 'descent' represents the *black work* of Hermeticism,[2] the solution of the solidification of the past, the release from the bonds of what is not, or, as *Advaita Vedānta* would say, the dissolution of all the 'veiling super-impositions' (*adhyāsa*). The being, in time and space, has projected into its psychical spatiality impulses of energy (ideas, feelings, desires, expectations, ways of behaving,

---

[1] G. Colli, *La sapienza greca*, op. cit. (Italics are ours).

[2] For this stage, see *The Threefold Pathway of Fire* by Raphael, op. cit., especially the Chapter 'Rectifying the common fires (*nigredo*)'.

and so on) which have then solidified, crystallised.[1] The ego, by identifying itself with these contents, is forced into becoming, never finding itself in its rightful place or time. In other words, it never experiences its state of the eternal present.

Today we may understand the term 'underworld' through the concept of the *subconsciousness*. This is our 'cellar', where we store qualities or, rather, solidified nuclei of qualities which restrain and constrain the reflection of the embodied Soul.

These nuclei are formed from the substance/matter (Plato would say χώρα) or the negative/receptive polarity of which the Soul, which imparts movement to bodies, represents the other polarity. This substance therefore has a feminine nature, and this is why Orpheus (Soul) has to go down into the 'cellar', take Eurydice (the Soul's reflection which is imprisoned by the solidified substance), release her from the state of constriction, and bring her back to the light of the sun, that is, to re-establish her in pure awareness, so that duality is resolved.

It is interesting to note that Eurydice dies (the reflection of the Soul is thus stunned and put to sleep, as if dead), and Orpheus has to restore her to life and active awareness. Plato expresses all of this in the *myth of the cave*.[2]

This procedure represents only one part of the entire Orphic ascesis. However, it is not enough to resolve the individual subconsciousness, because there is the collective subconsciousness. The 'descent to the underworld' must be

---

[1] For a further enquiry into these processes, see *Beyond the illusion of the ego* by Raphael, especially the Chapters regarding the birth and the solution of the coagulates of energy. Aurea Vidyā, New York.

[2] See *Politéia*, 514-517 and the Chapter 'Platonic ascent', in *Initiation into the Philosophy of Plato*, where Raphael presents 'the myth of the cave' from the point of view of Traditional Knowledge.

complete: it must embrace the lower world in its entirety. This implies that the Soul must also be released from all that humanity – as an individualised process – has crystallised. This is why the person who is going to be initiated is advised to remain deaf to the stimulations which come from the requirements of society. This is not easy, because different kinds of idealism and sentimentality hinder one from being *steadfast* in equanimity. On the other hand, the Orphic initiate is told that, as Soul, he does not belong to this world, for his true abode is divine. This world is nothing but a crystallised past which is perpetuated by the thrust which individualised man wishes to impart to it.

Vedānta would say that this solidified world is nothing but accumulated *karma*; it has no intrinsic, absolute reality of its own, no ipseity; the next *manvantara* (cosmic cycle) is nothing but the unresolved *karma* of the present *manvantara*.

There are two variants of the 'myth', and it is good to speak about them because they are of particular importance. According to one version, Orpheus, after winning over the divinities of the underworld with his divine singing, failed in his undertaking because he violated the condition not to turn back during the journey, on which he had to go in front of Eurydice, and she had to walk and follow in the footsteps of Orpheus.

According to another version, the powers of the underworld, realising that Orpheus lacked the necessary qualifications[1] to bring the undertaking to fulfilment, projected merely an image/shadow of Eurydice, while keeping her back in the depths of the underworld.

---

[1] Cf. the Chapter 'Qualifications of the disciple' in, *Awakening* by Raphael. Aurea Vidyā, New York.

Thus there are three states in which the initiate-to-be may find himself. The one just mentioned presents itself when he undertakes rectification without the necessary qualifications: the subconsciousness recognises this and creates false images, excuses, and more, in order to turn aside the unwitting aspirant. This is the state of some who believe they have achieved rectification or the solution of their own crystallised past, while in truth they are living on illusions and shadows; they believe, but are not. In other words, they have brought back from the underworld only the mental projection of their true self.

The state immediately prior to this is very painful, because the initiate-to-be may have certain qualifications, the right orientation, and an intelligent goodwill, but within him there is still some 'guardian of the threshold' which prevents him from truly turning his back on his past and on the individual and collective subconsciousness. If one goes into the *cave* to regain one's own *gold*, one must have all the determination, ability, and courage not to 'turn round'. One change of mind, one weakness, one excuse, one qualification with which one has lived for such a long time, one unbroken thread of *karma*, is enough to make the *opus* fail. This state is experienced by disciples who, though they have good intentions and good initiatory quali-fications, have not taken the process of purification to its completion. And we know that Orphism considers the pre-paratory stage of purification to be extremely important, as it constitutes, in fact, the first stage of the ascent. Indeed, those who are affiliated to the *Orphic Order* must live the 'Orphic life' (this is how Plato expresses it) which consists in observing certain norms of psychical and physical purity. The Orphists even have their own cemeteries where they cremate their deceased associates. Here are some passages from Plato which speak of purification.

'Well, my friend,' said Socrates, 'if this is true, anyone who reaches where I am going has a good hope of attaining there, in its fullness (and certainly nowhere else), that for which we have greatly exerted ourselves throughout our life; so that this departure, which is now ordained for me, is not without sweet hope, too, for anyone else who considers that his spirit has been prepared for it as if through *purification.*'

'Exactly', said Simmias.

'And is not *purification*, therefore, as it was described in the word of old [the reference is clearly to the 'sacred word' of the Orphists. Catharsis is the central idea of Orphism, an idea which was accepted and partially modified by the Pythagoreans], that is, to do one's utmost in every way to keep the soul separate from the body and accustom it to collecting itself and enclosing itself within itself, away from every bodily [titanic] element, remaining as much as possible – in this present life as well as in the life to come – utterly alone within oneself, intent on being liberated from the body, as if from chains?"[1]

'We see, in fact, that in many places men persist, even today, in sacrificing other men, and we learn, by contrast, that in other places there was a time when they did not dare to taste even oxen; their offerings to the gods consisted not of animals but of cakes, of fruits dipped in honey, and other innocent gifts of this kind; and they abstained from flesh, holding that it was not lawful to partake of it or to stain the altars of the gods with blood; in short, those men at that time lived the

---

[1]   Plato, *Phaedo*, 67 b-c-d. (Square brackets are ours).

special life which is called Orphic, making use of all that is lifeless but abstaining from all that has life.'[1]

The first state, by contrast, pertains to one who knows how to carry off the victory over his own crystallised shadows. Eurydice, chained by time and space, must be set free and released into the timelessness of that which has no space.

We need, moreover, to bear in mind that the initiate-to-be is being subjected to an Initiation, that is, to a 'complex ritual with the aim of introducing him, through successive stages, to an unusual experience. The task entrusted to the sacred families of the Eumolpides and the Kerykes, who governed the celebration of the Mysteries, consisted therefore, in its culminating aspect, in making a selection. Broadly speaking, the Initiation took place on two occasions, six months apart, by means of the Lesser Mysteries (celebrated in Spring at Agra) and the Greater Mysteries ... And finally the highest stage of the Mysteries, the *epoptéia*, which could not be attained until a year had passed after the initiation into the Greater Mysteries. Our sources are not clear about what was required from one who wished to be admitted to the *epoptéia*, but it is thought that here, at the apex of a procedure that has all the appearances of being selective, the number of the chosen would not be high ...

'After all, to confirm the thesis of a rigorous selection process there is the fundamental precept enfolding the Eleusinian occurrence: absolute secrecy, declared emphatically by the *Hymn to Demeter* and kept inviolate for a thousand years, until the malicious and incomplete revelations made by the Christian writers.'[2]

---

[1] ·Plato, *Laws*, 782 c.

[2] G. Colli, *La sapienza greca*, op. cit.

Demeter and Persephone are thought to have presided over the Lesser Mysteries at Eleusis, while Dionysus would have presided over the Greater Mysteries and the final *epoptéia*.

'On the rough torch-lit banks
Where, for mortal men, the ladies
Are foster mothers of the Holy Mysteries,
Whose key of gold is on the tongue
Of the Eumolpidean priests.'[1]

'But I have had the privilege of seeing
The magical rites of the initiates.'[2]

'And yet it is lawful that only the intellect of the philosopher should regain its wings, for he, as far as is possible, has his mind ever fixed on these objects [the solution of the individual subconsciousness] by means of which God is divine, because He is in continual communion with them. And the man who avails himself of these memories, being initiated into the perfect Mysteries, is the only one to become perfect. Having detached himself from human cares [solution of the collective unconscious] and adhering to the divine, he is considered mad by the crowd, which fails to realise that he is, indeed, possessed by God.'[3]

'O truly sacred Mysteries! O pure light! By the light of the torches I have an epoptic (ἐποπτικός)[4] vision of Heaven and of God. I am made pure by the Initiation. The Lord is the Hierophant who reveals the Mysteries; he marks the Initiate with his seal, lights his way, and

---

[1]   Sophocles, *Oedipus at Colonus*, 1049-1053.

[2]   Euripides, *Heracles*, 613.

[3]   Plato, *Phaedrus*, 249 c-d. (Square brackets are ours).

[4]   Epoptic: concerning the Mysteries, especially those at Eleusis.

commends him, because he has believed, to the care of God, by whom he will be protected in the time to come.'[1]

There is no doubt that Pythagoras, Parmenides, Empedocles, Sophocles, Euripides, Plato, Plutarch, Apuleius, and others, were initiated into the Greater Mysteries, and some of them even into the *epoptéia*.

The other 'myth' refers to the dismemberment of Orpheus by the Bacchantes and is connected to the 'myth' about the dismemberment of Dionysus himself; that is, the death and rebirth of God. There are two ways of analysing it: ritualistic and metaphysical. The first way, in turn, has two aspects: one is strictly ritualistic and views the rite as a *repetition of subjective and objective acts capable of producing particular effects*; the other consists in the right use of *sound* as the means of creating *harmony*. Of course, these two ways are not distinct, separate, or in opposition.

With regard to the first, we may say that Orphic ritualism is centred primarily on the death/rebirth of Dionysus; the Christian would say on the 'Passion'. This is why it is represented as a dramatic sequence in which we may see the death of God/Zagreus and his resurrection.

The *mystes*[2] must re-live this sequence, internalise it, and absorb it into his consciousness until all his faculties become one with the event. It is the neophyte himself who, having fallen to this plane of generation, must be reborn and wake up; and Dionysus, who represents the ever-living symbol of this event, offers himself as the strength, the influence, the grace that are required for spiritual rebirth.

---

[1] Clement of Alexandria, *Protreptikos pros Hellenas* (Hortatory Address to the Greeks), XII. 92.

[2] Mystes: *mystae* or *mystai*: an initiate in a Mystery (as in the Eleusinian Mysteries). Merriam-Webster.

The 'myth' of death/rebirth is therefore a very precise experience which must involve the deepest layers of consciousness rather than the simple emotional sphere. In other words, it must involve the being itself in its very essence. Only in this way does it become cathartic. For example, identifying with the 'Passion' of Jesus can produce the stigmata in the neophyte, or, indeed, as was the case with Therese Neuman, can lead to a conscious re-living of the entire sequence of the 'Passion'.

Now, one fact must be borne in mind: if the neophyte is not ready because he lacks fire, *eros*, aspiration for death/rebirth, the event that is represented cannot produce its due effects. If sufficient fuel, a consciousness yearning for identity with God, or a right relationship with the ritual act are missing, then this act may turn into a mere theatrical or folklore presentation. At the culminating moment of the rite, the qualified *mystes* undergo the 'breaking of the level of ego' and not only see, but also recognise, what they really are; that is, they recognise and re-discover themselves as Dionysus. In the words of *Vedānta*, they may be said to enter *samādhi*. The rite is a magic power which, if properly appreciated and followed, produces precise effects. The priestly art consists also in being able to comprehend the rite, and make use of it.

The 'myth', which is the symbol of an event, of a fact, contains a particular sequence, a precise format, which relates to its esoteric reality. It is therefore something that is lived; in it the *mystes* must find the clue, the way to follow, the goal to reach. The 'myth' of Dionysus says that he is torn to pieces by the Titans, to be put together again by Zeus. In the same way the neophyte, dashed to pieces (multiplicity) through his fall into generation, must be born anew to the Dionysian element and re-member himself in order to re-discover himself as metaphysical unity. The titanic element has split the unity, broken the equilibrium and the primordial harmony, and so he must die to this separative element and be born anew to the primordial unity.

Given this reality, the unity with the god is realised by following the course taken by the god: 'What Thou art, I shall be', 'What Thou hast done, I shall do.' This need for identity is not just a formality; it is real: the death/rebirth of the god is the means and the end at the same time, because the action of the *mystes* relies on the event, on what happened to the God, and leads to identity with the God himself.

Some ideas that were expressed earlier are repeated here: this identity may be incomplete, and in such a case there is an identification which is purely formal and in which neither the consciousness nor the psyche takes part; this may result in a caricature of the event, an outward imitation which is no more than a mere parody.

Again, there may be a mental or psychological imitation, as a result of which the *mystes* could believe he has attained identity when in fact this is not the case. He is a false initiate, though often in good faith. Some believe themselves to be what in reality they are not. Identification has occurred only with a projected form/image custom-made by one's own ego/mind.

On the other hand, there may be true identity, as a result of which there occurs an authentic transformation, conversion, turning round (περιαγωγή) of one's very being, from which one is born to a new state of consciousness. Being born anew into the God/Dionysus, the *mystes* is, of course, transfigured by escaping from the cycle of generation.

'I reached the frontier of death. Having crossed the threshold of Proserpina, I was led through all the elements, and then I made the return. In the middle of the night I saw a sun resplendent with bright light: I presented myself before the supernal gods and the deities of the underworld and I worshipped them close at hand.'[1]

'Having reached death, the soul feels a sensation like that experienced by the Initiates into the Greater Mysteries. In fact, the term 'to die' (*teleutai*) and the term 'to be initiated' (*teleisthai*) are similar, as are the two events themselves.

First of all, there is the wandering – wearying and endless – through the darkness [this is the passage from one plane to the next, characterised by darkness], and when the darkness disappears, striking things are seen [*bardo*]; then one shivers and trembles, sweats and fears. After that, a wondrous light is met with, and the soul finds itself in pure places where voices are heard, with the solemnity of sacred melodies, and dances and holy apparitions appear before the eyes.'[2]

'However, I am acquainted with a very effective Orphic rite, by means of which *fire rises* spontaneously towards the *head* and consumes from below the *one-eyed son* of the earth.'[3]

These passages are very significant and illuminating for those who have intuition and are acquainted with initiatory matters.

---

[1]   Apuleius, *Metamorphoses*, 11, 23.

[2]   Plutarch, *Moralia, fragment* 178. (Square brackets are ours).

[3]   Euripides, *Cyclops*, 646-648. (Italics are ours).

'Orpheus gave us the Initiations and taught us to abstain from killing. Musaeus, in turn, taught us the oracles and showed us how cure all illnesses completely.'[1]

'Here Plato is alluding to the Orphic Myths, according to which Dionysus is torn to pieces by the Titans and brought back to life by Apollo. This is why he says "to re-collect oneself and to enclose oneself within oneself", meaning to pass from the titanic life to the unitary life. Kore, too, is carried into Hades, but is brought back to the light by Demeter to live where she lived before.'[2]

De Santillana writes: 'Orpheus and his excruciating death could have been a poetic creation which emerged on many occasions in different places. But when characters who play the flute rather than the lyre end up being flayed alive for absurd reasons of various kinds, and when their identical end is repeatedly evoked in different continents, then we feel that we have got our hands on something, since similar accounts cannot be linked together through their inner sequence. And when the magic piper appears in the medieval German myth of Hamelin, or in Mexico long before the Conquest, and in both of the places is given certain attributes such as the colour red, it is very difficult to treat this as a coincidence. Usually there are very few things which get into music purely by chance. And so it is surely not an accident that numbers such as 108, or 9 x13, are repeated, in various multiples, in the *Vedas*, in

---

[1]   Aristophanes, *Frogs*, 1032-1033

[2]   Olympiodorus, *Commentary on the Phaedo of Plato*, 67 c.

the temples of Angkor, in Babylonia, in the obscure say-
ings of Heraclitus, and even those of the Norse Baköll.'

For the second mode of the first aspect, we recall that
Orpheus is a 'singer' and he plays on the lyre, with which
he enchants men, beasts, and gods. On account of being a
musician, he is also considered to be the son of Apollo.
It is natural to think that Orpheus, through his lyre, can
play notes which correspond to *states* of consciousness.

The lyre is not something simply to give amusement
or pass the time; the Tradition tells us that, by playing the
lyre, Orpheus tames wild beasts, enchants men, and speaks
to the gods. This implies that, through *sound*, he can put
himself in harmony with life and with beings.

We recall that Pythagoras draws from Orphism not so
much the ritual aspect as this musical direction and with
the monochord succeeds in discovering the 'Harmony of
the Spheres'. But Orpheus is the one who gives the precise
indications of the connection between sound/vibration and
the rhythm of life.

Apollo's lyre itself is not an object of pure pleasure,
for it has no need of any such thing, but it constructs the
worlds through precise tonal *relationships*. Kṛṣṇa, too, is
shown in the attitude of playing the flute. The manifest
universe is the synthesis of Number (quantity), Sound, and
Light; of vibration/quality and colour;[2] and Orpheus knows
this law and the way to apply it at particular levels of
existence.

Some men of devotion and learning - such as Ficino,
Pico della Mirandola, Agrippa, and so on - consider
Orpheus to be the greatest priestly Magus, who, by means
of Number, Dignity of rank, and the right instruments,

---

[1] G. de Santillana, *Hamlet's Mill*, op. cit.

[2] See the Chapter 'Vibrating life' in *Beyond Doubt*, by Raphael, op. cit.

can attract the divine Quality or the spiritual influence, especially in the Higher Initiations.

F. A. Yates writes: 'Ficino's Orphic magic [spiritual, natural, or priestly Magic] was a return to an ancient *priscus theologus* ... Orpheus comes second after Hermes in the Ficinian lists of *prisci theologi*.'

'He [Hermes Trismegistus] is said to be the first author of Theology: next after him was Orpheus, second among the Theologians of antiquity; Aglaophemus, who had been initiated into the sacred Teachings of Orpheus, had, as his successor in Theology, Pythagoras, one of whose disciples was Philolaus, master of our divine Plato. Thus there is an ancient Theology (*prisca theologia*) ... which has its origin in Hermes and its apogee in the divine Plato.'[1]

'The collection of hymns known as the *Orphica*... was the main source ... known to the Renaissance ... Ficino and his contemporaries believed that the Orphic Hymns were by Orpheus himself and were of extreme antiquity, reflecting the religious character of a *priscus magus* who lived long before Plato. Ficino's revival of Orphic Hymns singing has deep importance for him because he believes he is returning to the practice of a most ancient theologian and one who foresaw the Trinity.'[2]

Here is how Pico della Mirandola expresses himself in one of his *Conclusiones orphicae*:

'For the operations of natural magic nothing is more efficacious than the *Hymns* of Orpheus, provided that one applies the appropriate music, the right intention

---

[1] Marsilio Ficino, *Argumentum* on *Pimander*.

[2] F. A. Yates, *Giordano Bruno and the Hermetic Tradition*. The University of Chicago Press 1991.

of the mind, and all the other circumstances known to the wise.'

'The names of the gods as sung by Orpheus are not the names of deceitful demons, from whom comes evil, not good; but they are the names of divine powers or energies distributed in the cosmos by the true God, for the specific use of the man who knows how to avail himself of them.'[1]

Agrippa, treating of Orphic magic, writes:

'When Orpheus is writing to Musaeus, he enumerates the various divinities and gives them names, descriptions, and functions, invoking each one in turn in the hymns which he has dedicated to them. There is no need to believe that these names refer to malevolent and deceitful demons, but one should accept that they are appellations of *divine* and natural *powers*, ordained by the Eternal for the use of those men who know how to avail themselves of them.'[2]

Ficino emphasises that it is necessary to practise *magia naturalis*, spiritual or priestly magic, which is good, useful, and necessary, and not that demonic magic which is unlawful, perverse, and of a lower order.

Through the *science of sound*, Orpheus, like the Vedic *Ṛṣis* of old, calls divine Beings into the sanctuary so that they may function as 'Soul', as Archetype in the rites and sensible forms. The principial qualities, Uranus/Gaia, are reflected in the universal Soul, Chronos/Rhea, and, through Zeus, Ordainer of the world, they are reflected further in the sphere of the solid sensible.

---

[1] G. Pico della Mirandola, *Conclusiones orphicae*, X, 2-3, op. cit.

[2] Cornelius Agrippa, *Occult Philosophy*, Book 2. (Italics are ours).

Now, sound (consider the efficacy of the Vedic *mantras*) has the potential to penetrate into the intermediary world and attract Qualities, or Influences, of the intelligible order and to channel them, for instance, into a Temple or an Initiation rite.

A sound, a *maṇḍala*, a *yantra*, and the rite itself can constitute *sounding vessels* by means of which Influences originating from the universal are transmitted. A form – be it corporeal or of any other nature – deteriorates because it lacks the divine *influence* on which it depends; through the agency of these *sounding vessels* the form can be activated and restored.

A traditional Form, for example, can also deteriorate in time/space, either through lack of people qualified in the Teaching or through elements that have been introduced without the appropriate psychological qualities and the adequate level of consciousness.

Out of consideration for this state of affairs, some great Souls *manifest* themselves from the intelligible plane into the sensible plane by acting as *sounding vessels* (hence the exalted figures of Hermes, Orpheus, Pythagoras, Plato, Śaṅkara, Buddha, and so forth) and, by transmitting the *influence* of the intelligible world, they succeed in rectifying the Form, unless the Form has fulfilled its function and needs to be withdrawn and 'abstracted'.

In this way the authentic Priest plays an extremely important and divine rôle: by acting as a bridge between the intelligible and the sensible, he keeps the vital circuit open. This can happen because the cosmos does not have separate compartments but is an indivisible unity.

The other aspect of the 'myth' is more of a metaphysical order. As we have noted before, this symbolism, which is not, of course, exclusive to Orphism, enables us to understand how the principal Unity, by making divisions of itself, is polarised into the same number of unities, thus giving rise to multiplicity.

Thus it comes about that the One, by polarising itself, *appears* as two (the sum of *one* and *one*), two *appears* as three (*one* plus *one* plus *one*), and three *appears* as four. If we add these unities, the daughters of Unity/Principle, we obtain the number nine (the number of perfect Initiation), and if we include Unity/Principle we have ten, which represents whole and complete perfection; and according to *Qabbālāh*, ten is the number of the *Sephirots*, because the *Ain Soph* is transcendent.[1]

We said that the One *appears* as two, not that the One transforms itself or changes into two, and there is a philosophical consideration here.

The One, if it is truly such, cannot change its nature and transform itself into two or some other nature. The nature of the One, as Reality/Principle, cannot betray itself, cannot change its nature, because, if it did, the manifestation which has objectivised would collapse. Two, three, and so on, exist and have their *raison d'être* because the One abides in its constant reality.

We may say that the One represents the foundation on which multiplicity can exist and be what it is. But while there can be no multiplicity without the One, because multiplicity has no *raison d'être* within itself, the One, by contrast, abides even without multiplicity.

The One, therefore, may *appear* as two, three, and so forth, but in reality it underlies every number without suffering any diminution. It represents the substratum and essence *in abscondito* of the numerical sequence. *Vedānta*

---

[1] For further insights and especially for the metaphysical aspect of *Ain Soph*, see the Chapter 'The Metaphysical Pathway' in *Pathway of Fire according to the Qabbālāh*, by Raphael. Aurea Vidyā, New York.

would say that *Brahman appears* as the manifold world but is *not* the manifold world. The One is *not* two, three, and so on; the One is always one and will always be one, and it cannot be other than one since that is its nature.

Although the mind (this is only an analogy) can project countless data (especially in dreams), yet it remains the same mind without exhausting itself in the apparent multiplicity which it has conceived.

Now, Orphism seems to tell us that you are the immortal Soul, you are not this body/prison. Although you may consider yourself to be the body/prison to the point of forgetting your real nature, you will always remain the immortal Soul. In annihilating yourself as the Soul, in estranging yourself from the Soul, in alienating yourself from your authentic state of existence, in splintering your being, you find 'death' (Dionysus, who is torn to pieces) and you also find your conflict and your 'suicide'.

If you wish to escape from this scissure, from this *oblivion* (a Platonic term, but the basis of the Orphic vision), from this prostrating and obscuring alienation, you must set out on the path of return, of conversion, and in this you can be guided by the Orphic Knowledge, the Orphic Mysteries, and the Orphic 'life-style'.

Here is a very significant passage from Plotinus:

'Intelligence (νοῦς) is therefore eternally undivided and unbroken; and the soul, too, is undivided and unbroken up above; but it is possible for the nature of the soul to be divided (δὲ φύσιν μερίζεσθαι). Its division consists in departing from above and coming into a body. It is rightly said that it "is divided within bodies", for in this way the soul distances itself and divides itself. Then how can it remain also "undivided"? This is because it does not distance itself in its entirety,

for there is a part of it which has not come down
here since its nature cannot be divided. To say that
the soul "is composed of an indivisible essence and
a divisible essence within bodies" is to say, therefore,
that it consists of an essence which remains above
and of another essence which comes down here and
depends on the other essence and moves here like a
radius from the centre."[1]

Union with one's own Daimon can be effected after
the stage of preliminary purification, which, according to
Plato in his reference to Orphism, means separating the
soul from the body, and this can happen after the 'descent
to the underworld', but not before. Moreover, with reference
to the purification it should be made clear that the original
Orphists lived in segregated initiatory communities, wore
special white garments, observed many norms and prohi-
bitions, and had their own cemeteries. The 'Orphic life'
is permeated by consistent norms, all aimed at dissolving
identification with the titanic element.

We noted earlier that Orphic institutions prefer the
heights, while 'lunar' institutions prefer valleys. Many factors contribute to this situation; for example, the masses
of humanity, as such, release powerful currents of energy
which is qualified by heavy, individualised vibration/radia-
tion; this coarse current of vibration has a negative impact
on sensitive organisms which are trying to raise the notes,
the tones, the rhythms.

The problem can also be expressed in different terms:
the collective unconscious is a powerful *qualified force*
which exerts an influence on the psyche of an individual.
Human potential in its wholeness – like sunspots, the

---

[1] Plotinus, *Enneads*, IV, 2, I. See also II, 9, II; IV, 3, XII; IV, 8, IV,
op. cit.

full moon, and so on – influences the basic functions of sensitive organisms. All passions are whirlpools of forces produced by the same number of life-whirlpools; we need to recognise that a specific manifest field is the play of influences which attracts or repels whatever is near it. A person, a planet, and so on, constitutes a centre, a vibrational point/vortex, which can have a positive or negative influence on other living systems. Those that are not sensitive are not aware of this, but that does not prevent the phenomenon from existing all the same.

Then there is another aspect regarding purification. In the centres at Eleusis and Delphi, before the arrival of Orphism, purification was prescribed for just a few days prior to the neophyte's Initiation, but the Orphists proposed the practice of purification as a norm of life. Union with one's own Daimon cannot be realised without this steadfast and continuous purification, an additional reason being that the lack of purification prevents the total dissolution of the lower/titanic world.

If Orphism professes a firm belief in the immortal Soul and the equally firm belief in its 'fall', it follows that the ultimate aim of the 'Orphic life' must be to 're-unite that which has been scattered' and forgotten.[1] If one is Immortal Soul, and the Soul by its nature is free from bodily materiality, then the Orphic neophyte has no other goal, no other aim, no other aspiration, except that of re-discovering himself in that which really is. All the rest – every possible worldly experience, however noble and extraordinary – can represent nothing but an increasingly greater estrangement from one's own true nature. Every individualised experience is undergone by the *shadow* of

---

[1] See Aphorism 41 of the Chapter 'The Fire of Life' in *The Threefold Pathway of Fire*, op. cit.

the true being, which makes the reality of the Daimon ever more obscure. Every externalisation is simply losing oneself in something other, depending on something other, which may be called a non-being.

The philosophical reflection which originated from Thales onwards is due to Orphism and not to the Homeric conception of life. The Mysteries arose with Orpheus, and consequently the Western initiatory Tradition derives from Orpheus. One belief is that Orpheus lived at the time of Moses and that both were initiated within the sacred Egyptian temples, coming forth with unusual treasures of knowledge and realisation. Through its affinity with the Eastern Teachings, Orphism, like the *Upaniṣads*, required the whole being to be 'torn away' from the titanic contingency and raised to the peaks of metaphysical reality, and this would seem to have run counter to the various spiritual views of its time. In fact, Orpheus – and therefore Orphism – aimed not only at tearing man away from the contingent and re-uniting him with his own immortal Daimon, but also at integrating the Daimon itself with the celestial Dionysus, who is of a universal metaphysical order. This is why it was noted earlier that purification and the 'descent to the underworld' may represent only one stage of the Orphic realisative journey, rather than the final goal.

Here we can discover two aspects of extraordinary importance; the first comes from recognising that Orpheus is speaking in terms of the Greater Mysteries, and the second from recognising that the Soul, or Daimon, belongs to the same nature as Dionysus, which means that there is solution by *identity* and not just 'salvation' for the Daimon, which, even when saved, always remains a Daimon. 'From man [soul] you will be re-born as God.' The first aspect is linked to the second.

Orpheus proclaimed the *identity* of the human Soul with the divine Soul, and this truth, it should be noted, is also expressed by the *Upaniṣads*. All the various post-Orphic Western religious forms express themselves not in terms of *Identity* but in terms of duality: Creator, creature. It could well be said that the Orphic Tradition was the first to propose a genuinely metaphysical vision; or rather, one could even believe that it is non-dual (*advaita*), since it holds as real and absolute only the supreme Being, of which Dionysus is a universal representation. And without Orpheus, Parmenides could not have conceived the supreme Being (Orphism expanded with outstanding success in Sicily and in *Magna Graecia* in general), and Plato could not have conceived the intelligible world or the One Good.

Proclus states:

> 'What Orpheus taught by means of esoteric allegories is what Pythagoras taught, after being initiated into the Orphic Mysteries, and what Plato taught through the Orphic Mysteries and the actual writings of the Pythagoreans.'[1]

The Mysteries which might have existed at the time of Orpheus were not the genuine Mysteries: they were directed only at purifying the emotions and obtaining some contingent aspect, their character being primarily naturalistic. But with Orpheus there was a release of outstanding quality, at both the cognitive and the practical levels. The same thing happened in India with Gauḍapāda and Śaṅkara, who, from the *Vedas/Upaniṣads*, developed the highest form of spirituality, in contrast to the reductive, pragmatic religiosity of the ritualism found in the *Karma Mimāṁsā*.

---

[1] Proclus, *Platonic Theology*, I, 6, 13.

It is also worth noting that although the Mosaic *Book of Genesis* considers man to have been created in the image of God, and although it gives man power over all the sub-human creatures, it does not say that man/Adam, even before his 'fall', is a divine being by nature: he is just born of the dust of the earth. According to the Orphic vision, however, the human Soul is divine, a reflection of Dionysus himself, having the very nature of Zeus; and this nature is restored by transcending the titanic element. The 'fall' of Orphic man is always a fall of a contingent order.

The Orphic teaching and ascent are encountered, too, in the Tradition of Hermes Trismegistus:

> 'And so, O Asclepius, man is a *magnum miraculum*, a being worthy of reverence and honour. For he approaches the divine nature as if he were himself a god, and he is familiar with the race of the gods, knowing how to share his origin with them. He despises that part of his nature which is merely human, because he has placed his hope in the divinity of the other part of himself.'[1]

---

[1] *Asclepius*, 6.

INNOVATIVE ASPECTS OF THE ORPHIC MYSTERIES

The 'innovations' of Orphism which regard spheres of the intelligible, the sensible, and the ethical as a 'lifestyle' in Greek society can be summarised in the following points:

1. Positing an Intelligible sphere beyond the sensible sphere. This has been made use of by all the initiated Philosophers from Pythagoras to Parmenides, Plato, and others.

2. Presenting the idea of a supreme, transcendental Principle, as opposed to the immanentist and pluralistic conception found in the Homeric view. This has been used particularly by Parmenides and Plato, and later by Christianity itself. Here is a fragment in which this idea is expounded:

'Zeus was born first, Zeus of the flashing thunderbolt last;
Zeus is the beginning, Zeus is the middle: by Zeus all is accomplished;
Zeus is the upholder of the Earth and the starry Heavens;
Zeus was born male, immortal Zeus was a girl;
Zeus is the breath of all things, Zeus is the impulse of the untameable Fire;
Zeus is the root of the sea, Zeus is the sun and the moon;
Zeus is the King, Zeus of the flashing thunderbolt is the Lord of all things;

Indeed, having concealed all things, from his sacred heart he brought them forth anew to the joyful light, fulfilling arduous enterprises.'[1]

Another Orphic fragment quoted by Plato says:

'The god [Zeus], as say the words of old, "who holds the beginning, the end, and the middle of all the things that are".'[2]

This fragment undoubtedly reminds us of the *Upaniṣadic* vision; it is enough simply to refer to a *sūtra* or two from the *Māṇḍūkya Upaniṣad*:

'*Om* is all this ... [that which is] the past, the present, and the future is only *oṁkāra*. And that which transcends threefold time is also the syllable *Om*.'

'In truth, *praṇava* [as *Brahman*] is the beginning, the middle, and the end of everything.'[3]

3. Pointing out the existence of an immortal Soul in man, in contrast to the mere survival of shades in the Homeric tradition.

This was made use of by all the later initiatory Traditions, including Christianity. Cilento writes: 'Orphism, like Christianity, demands the whole man, tears him from his earthly roots, and transports him to a more breathable atmosphere.'[4]

---

[1]   See *fragment* 21 a [1] Kern, *Orfica*, op. cit.

[2]   Plato, *Laws* IV, 715 e-716 a. See also Aeschylus, *Heliades* ('The Daughters of the Sun'), *fragment* 48: 'Zeus is the air, Zeus is the earth, Zeus is the heaven, Zeus is all things and that, too, which is above all things.'

[3]   See Gauḍapāda, *Māṇḍūkyakārikā*, Chapter I, *sūtra* 1 and *kārikā* 27, edited by Raphael. Aurea Vidyā, New York.

[4]   V. Cilento, 'La mistica ellenica', in *La Mistica non Cristiana*, op. cit.

4. Proclaiming the traditional idea of the 'fall' of the Soul into the world of a corruptible generation/manifestation. With this there is posited, as a consequence, the problem of *good* and *evil* in man, and hence his direct responsibility to set about purifying the titanic element embodied within mortal nature.[1] Once again Christianity owes a debt to Orphism.

5. Offering Knowledge which is theoretical, practical, and ritualistic in such a way as to achieve unity with the Soul and then with the Divine itself. This is how Orphism instituted the initiatory procedure, no longer to propitiate some deity for personal egoistic goals (see the Hindu *Karma Mīmāṁsā* and Egyptian ritualism), but for realisative and purely initiatory purposes, by raising the Temples of Delphi, Eleusis, Thebes, Olympia, and others to true spiritual activity by means of the Greater and Lesser Mysteries.

The post-Orphic Western religions have been exoteric rather than esoteric.

6. Positing the *identity* of Soul and divine Principle. This is of fundamental importance in the Western initiatory Tradition. Man is God in potentiality.

7. Proclaiming the idea of transmigration and therefore of individual responsibility for actions undertaken. That which connects one to the world of deaths and rebirths (*saṁsāra* is the term used in *Vedānta*) is the *karma* or action which does not conform to the Principle (this represents the New Testament saying, 'Whatsoever a man soweth, that shall he also reap'[2]).

---

[1] For a further enquiry on the 'fall', see 'The "fall" of the Soul' in *The Pathway of Non-Duality*, by Raphael, op. cit.

[2] St Paul, *Letter to the Galatians*, 6:7.

8. Providing a code of initiatory ethics, not as an end in itself but as a means of effecting a catharsis and transfiguration of one's titanic nature. This is how the foundations were laid for a new type of *areté* in contrast to the traditional Homeric type. This system of ethics exercised a particularly strong influence on the Pythagorean school and the Platonic school.

9. As a result, Orphic *areté* played a part in modifying society itself with a new way of willing, thinking, and acting. In this context, *areté* (ἀρετή) corresponds to that characteristic by which a thing is what it has to be, that which represents its peculiarity; thus the *areté* of the Soul is to know.

This topic was fully developed by Plato.

10. Again, the foundation of Christianity is the 'Passion' of Jesus: death, rebirth, ascension to Heaven. It is the same in Orphism: the death of Orpheus, his rebirth, and his elevation to the Divinity of Zeus. See the words on page 42.

11. Finally with Orpheus the initiatory Tradition of the Mysteries became anchored in Europe, and therefore in the West, on a par with the Eastern tradition and the tradition in Egypt. Orpheus promotes the transcendental aspect rather than the physical/sensible aspect.

In India Gauḍapāda and Śaṅkara were the ones responsible for establishing genuine realisative metaphysics, with *Asparśavāda* and *Advaita Vedānta*, with which Orphism shares the same fundamental view, with neither borrowing from the other, because supreme Truth transcends space, time, and causality, and anyone who has realised it is untouched by factors of interference.

That Orpheus, in addition to being Priest of the Mysteries, was a traditional philosopher is confirmed by antiquity and our own times. So we should read these words of Colli, because they are extremely important:

'The suspicion that Orpheus was also a philosopher is confirmed later when, with regard to the first principles of another Orphic Theogony, that of Hieronymus and Hellanicus, we read: "Time was called ageless... and to him was conjoined Ananke, identical in nature to Adrasteia, bodiless and with arms that extended over all the world, even to its very ends". Time and Necessity: a pair of decisive categories. Here the wisdom of remotest antiquity can re-appear as a philosophy of today: in fact, the link of the sensible representations – that is, their principle – can truthfully claim to be called time, just as the link of the abstract representations – that is, their principle – can claim to be called necessity. And it cannot be denied that the abstract representations are "conjoined" to those that are sensible. But to return to Orpheus, if even Necessity – that is, Ananke – is a principle of appearance, which goddess is contrasted with her in the Mystery-place beyond appearance? Is it perhaps causality, fortune, that is, Tyche? Traces suggesting this meaning exist, but they are too faint ...

'On the other hand, the allusion to the mirror of Dionysus is esoteric, the mirror being one of the god's attributes which appear in the Mystery-ritual as a wisdom-symbol which the Orphic myth brings in at the culminating moment of the god's passion: "With hideous sword the Titans violated Dionysus, who was staring at the deceitful image in the alienating mirror."'[1]

Indeed, Proclus writes in his Commentary to the *Timaeus*:

---

[1] G. Colli. *La sapienza greca*. Op cit..

'And in ancient times the mirror was handed down by the theologians too, as the symbol of the adequacy of the intuitive perfection of the universe. This is why they also say that Hephaestus made a mirror for Dionysus and that the god, while looking into it and contemplating his own image, threw himself into creating multiplicity.'[1]

And here is Colli once more: 'The mirror is a symbol of illusion, because what we see in the mirror does not exist in reality, but is merely a reflection. [This symbol appears likewise in the Eastern Tradition, in *Vedānta* and Buddhism]. But the mirror is also a symbol of knowledge, because by looking at myself in the mirror I come to know myself. And this is purely in a refined sense, because all knowing is bringing the world into a mirror, reducing it to a *reflection* which I possess. And now here comes the thunderbolt of the Orphic image: Dionysus looks at himself in the mirror and sees the world! The themes of deceit and knowledge are conjoined, but it is in this way alone that they are resolved. The god is attracted by the mirror, by this toy where unknown multi-coloured images appear – the sight holds him fast, unaware of the danger – for he does not know that he is contemplating himself. And yet what he sees is the reflection of a god, *the way in which a god expresses himself in the world of appearance.*

'The antithesis between *appearance* and divinity [reality], between necessity and play, is resolved here in a single image, where everything splits and re-unites, where the vision illumines that which thought beclouds. *Dionysus alone exists*: we and our world are his deceptive *appearance*, that which he sees when he is before the mirror. [And this is what is indicated by the metaphysics

---

[1]   Proclus, *Commentary on the Timaeus of Plato*, 33 b.

of *Advaita Vedānta*: the two Traditions coincide perfectly, sometimes in the very wording] ... And then the knowledge becomes a norm of conduct, too: theory and practice merge. In fact, there is an ancient Orphic discourse which speaks of 'roads', the ones to follow and the ones to avoid, the ones of the Initiates and the ones of the worldly. The way [ὸδός], the path, is an image, an allusion, which recurs in the age of the wise, in Heraclitus, Parmenides, and Empedocles.[1]

According to *Advaita Vedānta*, only the *Brahman* is real: the universe/phenomenon is merely *appearance*. By means of māyā (the equivalent of the mirror in Orphism), *Brahman* appears as the universe.

It is the myth of Narcissus, who, while looking at himself in water, contemplates his own 'shadow' and, by identifying himself with it, forgets his true nature.[2]

According to Parmenides, Being alone *is*; the world is a mere appearance.

We can conclude this brief work, which may stimulate the reader to go more deeply into the matter, with a passage from the divine Plato:

'And those who instituted the Mysteries were far from foolish; and, in truth, ever since ancient times they have shown us, in a veiled way, that anyone who comes to Hades without being initiated and without being purified will lie in the mud; on the other hand, anyone who has been initiated and purified, on arriving there,

---

[1]   G. Colli. *La sapienza greca*, op. cit. (Italics and square brackets added).

With reference to the two 'roads' here is Gauḍapāda's *Māṇḍukyakārikā*, *kārikā* 90, Chapter IV: 'That which must be avoided, that which must be known, that which must be accepted and that which must be rendered ineffective must be clearly comprehended from the beginning.'

[2]   See Plotinus, *Enneads*, I, 6, VIII; IV, 3, XII.

will dwell with the gods. Indeed, those who interpret the Mysteries say that "the rod-bearers are many, but the Bacchuses are few". And these, I think, are those who rightly practised philosophy."[1]

---

[1]   Plato, *Phaedo*, 69 c-dc

HIPPONION GOLD TABLET*

---
* Ancient Greek text on the cover

This is the Work of Memory

*When you are about to die, you will go to the well-
made halls of Hades.*

*To the right is a spring, and next to it stands a
white cypress.*

*Coming down to that place, the souls of the dead
refresh themselves.*

Go nowhere near this spring.

*Ahead you will find clear water flowing forth from
the Lake of Memory*

*Over which stand guards, who with keen mind will
ask you*

What you truly seek in the gloom of deadly Hades.

Say, 'A child of earth and the starry Heaven,

I am parched with thirst and perishing;

*But quickly give me cool water flowing from the
Lake of Memory.'*

They will surely speak to the Queen below the earth

And will give you to drink of the Lake of Memory.

And then may you journey far on the Sacred Way

*Travelled by other renowned initiates and devotees
of Dionysus.*

RAPHAEL
Unity of Tradition

Raphael, having attained a synthesis of Knowledge (which is not associated with eclecticism or with syncretism), aims at 'presenting' the Universal Tradition in its many Eastern and Western expressions. He has spent a substantial number of years writing and publishing books on spiritual experience; his works include commentaries on the *Qabbālāh*, Hermeticism and Alchemy. He has also commented on and compared the Orphic Tradition with the works of Plato, Parmenides, and Plotinus. Furthermore, Raphael has written several books on the pathway of non-duality (*Advaita*). He has also translated and commented on a number of key Vedantic texts from the original Sanskrit.

With reference to Platonism, Raphael has highlighted the fact that, if we were to draw a parallel between Śaṅkara's *Advaita Vedānta* and a Traditional Western Philosophical Vision, we could refer to the Vision presented by Plato. Drawing such a parallel does not imply a search for reciprocal influences, but rather it points to something of paramount importance: a sole Truth, inherent in the doctrines (teachings) of several great thinkers who, although far apart in time and space, have reached similar and in some cases even identical conclusions.

One notices how Raphael's writings aim to manifest and underscore the Unity of Tradition from the metaphysical perspective. This does not mean that he is in opposition to a dualistic perspective, or to the various religious faiths, or 'points of view'.

An embodied real metaphysical Vision cannot be opposed to anything. What counts for Raphael is the unveiling, through living and being, which one has been able to contemplate.

In the light of the Unity of Tradition Raphael's writings or commentaries offer the intuition of the reader precise points of correspondence between Eastern and Western Teachings. These points of reference are useful for those who want to approach a comparative doctrinal study and to enter the spirit of the Unity of the Teaching.

For those who follow either the Eastern or the Western traditional line these correspondences help in comprehending how the *Philosophia Perennis* (Universal Tradition), which has no history and has not been formulated by human minds as such, 'comprehends universal truths that do not belong to any people or any age'. It is only for lack of 'comprehension' or 'synthetic vision' that one particular Branch is considered the only reliable one. From this position there can be only opposition and fanaticism. What degrades the Teaching is sentimental, fanatical devotionalism as well as proud intellectualism, which is critical and sterile, dogmatic and separative.

In Raphael's words: 'For those of us who aim at Realisation, our task is to get to the essence of every Teaching, because we know that, just as Truth is one, so Tradition is one even if, just like Truth, Tradition may be viewed from a plurality of apparently different points of view. We must abandon all disquisitions concerning the phenomenal process of becoming, and move onto the plane of Being. In other words, we must have a Philosophy of Being as the foundation of our search and of our realisation.'[1]

Raphael interprets spiritual practice as a 'Pathway of Fire'. Here is what he writes: 'The "Path of Fire" is the

---

[1] See Raphael, *Tat tvam asi*, (That thou art). Aurea Vidyā, New York

pathway which each disciple follows in all branches of the Tradition; it is the Way of Return. Therefore, it is not the particular teaching of an individual or the path parallel to the one and only Main Road... After all, every disciple follows his own "Path of Fire", no matter which Branch of the Tradition he belongs to'.

In Raphael's view, what is important is to express through living and being the truth that one has been able to contemplate. Thus, for each being, one's expression of thought and action must be coherent and in agreement with one's own specific *dharma*.

After more than 60 years of teaching, in both oral and written format, Raphael withdrew into *mahāsamādhi*.

* * *

May Raphael's Consciousness, an expression of Unity of Tradition, guide and illumine along this *Opus* all those who donate their *mens informalis* (non-formal mind) to the attainment of the highest known Realisation.

PUBLICATIONS

Aurea Vidyā Collection

1. Raphael, *The Threefold Pathway of Fire*, Thoughts that Vibrate for an Alchemical, Æsthetical, and Metaphysical ascesis
Retail ISBN 978-1-931406-00-0
Amazon   978-1-931406-00-0
Apple etal. 978-1-931406-46-8 forthcoming

2. Raphael, *At the Source of Life*, Questions and Answers concerning the Ultimate Reality
Retail ISBN 978-1-931406-01-7
Amazon   979-8-576124-75-6
Apple etal. 978-1-931406-32-1

3. Raphael, *Beyond the illusion of the ego*, Synthesis of a Realizative Process
Retail ISBN 978-1-931406-03-1
Amazon   978-1-931406-03-1
Apple etal. 978-1-931406-18-5 forthcoming

4. Raphael, *Tat tvam asi*, That thou art, The Path of Fire According to the Asparśavāda
Retail ISBN 978-1-931406-02-4
Amazon   979-8-583067-52-7
Apple etal. 978-1-931406-34-5

5. Gauḍapāda, *Māṇḍūkyakārikā*, The Metaphysical Path of *Vedānta**
Retail ISBN 978-1-931406-04-8
Amazon   978-1-931406-04-8
Apple etal. 978-1-931406-45-1 forthcoming

6. Raphael, *Orphism and the Initiatory Tradition*
Retail ISBN 979-8-539590-78-9
Amazon   978-1-931406-05-5
Apple etal.   978-1-931406-35-2

7. Śaṅkara, *Ātmabodha*, Self-knowledge*
Retail ISBN 978-1-931406-06-2
Amazon   978-1-931406-06-2
Apple etal.   978-1-931406-53-6 forthcoming

8. Raphael, *Initiation into the Philosophy of Plato*
Retail ISBN 978-1-931406-07-9
Amazon   978-1-466486-98-0
Apple etal.   978-1-931406-52-9

9. Śaṅkara, *Vivekacūḍāmaṇi*, The Crest-jewel of Discernment*
Retail ISBN 978-1-931406-08-6
Amazon   978-1-931406-08-6
Apple etal.   978-1-931406-48-2 forthcoming

10. *Dṛdṛśyaviveka*, A philosophical investigation into the nature of the 'Seer' and the 'seen'*
Retail ISBN 978-1-931406-09-3
Amazon   979-8-669178-69-7
Apple etal.   978-1-931406-28-4

11. Parmenides, *On the Order of Nature*, Περί φύσεως, For a Philosophical Ascesis*
Retail ISBN 978-1-931406-10-9
Amazon   979-8-698821-95-3
Apple etal.   978-1-931406-22-2

12. Raphael, *The Science of Love*, From the desire of the senses to the Intellect of Love
Retail ISBN 978-1-931406-12-3
Amazon   978-1-931406-12-3
Apple etal.   978-1-931406-54-3 forthcoming

13. Vyāsa, *Bhagavadgītā*, The Celestial Song*
Retail ISBN 978-1-931406-13-0
Amazon 979-8-562809-02-5
Apple etal. 978-1-931406-50-5

14. Raphael, *The Pathway of Fire according to the Qabbālāh* (Ehjeh 'Ašer 'Ehjeh), I am That I am
Retail ISBN 978-1-931406-14-7
Amazon 978-1-931406-14-7
Apple etal. 978-1-931406-49-9 forthcoming

15. Patañjali, *The Regal Way to Realization*, Yogadarśana*
Retail ISBN 978-1-931406-15-4
Amazon 978-1-931406-15-4
Apple etal. 978-1-931406-20-8

16. Raphael, *Beyond Doubt*, Approaches to Non-duality
Retail ISBN 978-1-931406-16-1
Amazon 979-8-657281-16-3
Apple etal. 978-1-931406-25-3

17. Bādarāyaṇa, *Brahmasūtra*
Retail ISBN 978-1-931406-17-8
Amazon 978-1-931406-17-8
Apple etal. 978-1-931406-47-5 forthcoming

18. Śaṅkara, *Aparokṣānubhūti*, Self-realization*
Retail ISBN 978-1-931406-23-9
Amazon 978-1-931406-19-2
Apple etal. 978-1-931406-30-7

19. Raphael, *The Pathway of Non-Duality*, Advaitavāda
Retail ISBN 978-1-931406-21-5
Amazon 979-8-552322-16-9
Apple etal. 978-1-931406-24-6

20. *Five Upaniṣads*, Īśa, Kaivalya, Sarvasāra, Amṛtabindu, Atharvaśira*
Retail ISBN 978-1-931406-26-0
Amazon   978-1-931406-26-0
Apple etal. 978-1-931406-29-1

21. Raphael, *The Philosophy of Being,* A conception of life for coming out of the turmoil of individual and social conflict
Retail ISBN 978-1-931406-27-7
Amazon   979-8-630006-39-4
Apple etal. 978-1-931406-31-4

22. Raphael, *Awakening*
Retail ISBN 978-1-931406-44-4
Amazon   979-8-716953-07-9
Apple etal. 978-1-931406-33-8

Related Publications

A brief biography, *Śaṅkara*
Aurea Vidyā. New York.
Retail ISBN 978-1-931406-11-6
Amazon   978-1-931406-11-6

Forthcoming Publications

Śaṅkara, *Short Works*, Treatises and Hymns*
Retail ISBN 978-1-931406-71-0
Amazon   978-1-931406-55-0
Apple etal. 978-1-931406-56-7

Māṇḍūkya Upaniṣad, with the Gauḍapāda's *kārikā*s and the Commentary of Śaṅkara*
Retail ISBN 978-1-931406-37-6
Amazon 978-1-931406-57-4
Apple etal. 978-1-931406-58-1

Upaniṣads*
Retail ISBN 978-1-931406-38-3
Amazon 978-1-931406-59-8
Apple etal. 978-1-931406-60-4

Raphael, *Essence and Purpose of Yoga*, The Initiatory Pathways to the Transcendent
Retail ISBN 978-1-931406-36-9
Amazon 978-1-931406-61-1
Apple etal. 978-1-931406-62-8

Self-knowledge, The Harmonization of Psychic Energy. Edited by the Kevala Group
Retail ISBN 978-1-931406-40-6
Amazon 978-1-931406-63-5
Apple etal. 978-1-931406-64-2

Uttaragītā*
Retail ISBN 978-1-931406-68-0
Amazon 978-1-931406-69-7
Apple etal. 978-1-931406-70-3

Sanskrit Glossary
Retail ISBN 978-1-931406-67-3
Amazon 978-1-931406-65-9
Apple etal. 978-1-931406-66-6

* Translation from Sanskrit or Greek and Commentary by Raphael.

Aurea Vidyā is the Publishing House of the Parmenides Traditional Philosophy Foundation, a Not-for-Profit Organization whose purpose is to make Perennial Philosophy accessible.

The Foundation goes about its purpose in a number of ways: by publishing and distributing Traditional Philosophy texts with Aurea Vidyā, by offering individual and group encounters and by providing a Reading Room and daily Meditations at its Center.

* * *

Those readers who have an interest in Traditional Philosophy are welcome to contact the Foundation at: parmenides.foundation@earthlink.net.

www.ingramcontent.com/pod-product-compliance
Lightning Source LLC
Chambersburg PA
CBHW032229080426
42735CB00008B/772